"Few people are poised to write a book about the power of customer service, creativity, and excellence, but Mike Kai is at the top of that list. I know Mike best as the pastor of one of the most influential churches in Hawai'i, but with his background in the airline industry, restaurant industry, and general business and nonprofit spaces, Mike has learned the secret to adaptation and creating a culture of excellence. In *That Doesn't Just Happen*, he provides you the tools to make an impact and increase your influence wherever you find yourself."

—JOHN C. MAXWELL, *New York Times* Bestselling Author

"Mike Kai possesses something rare, even among great leaders: not only the combination of a remarkable vision, but also understanding the details to make that vision happen. His new book, *That Doesn't Just Happen*, is an incredibly insightful look at how both abilities working together create the greatest breakthroughs. Whatever your vision and whatever your dream, this book is for you. It will teach you a unique set of principles that will transform your leadership."

—PHIL COOKE, PH.D., Filmmaker, Media Consultant, and author of *Maximize Your Impact: How to Make Digital Media Work for Your Church, Your Ministry, and You*

"In this timely and necessary work, my friend Mike Kai challenges leaders to raise the bar and intentionally provide the kind of care and service that is reflective of God's love for his people. Although he uses Solomon as a model for leadership, the heart of this book points us to the example set by Jesus, who is the ultimate expression of amazing service and inimitable leadership."

—DR. DHARIUS DANIELS, Lead Pastor of Change Church and author of *Relational Intelligence*

"That Doesn't Just Happen is an incredible book and resource for us all. In a time where people are searching for leaders that are genuine, loving, intentional, and grace-filled, Mike shares what it takes to build an organization and culture that reflects those values. I want to encourage you to lean in as you read this book, take notes, and put into practice these principles!"

—CHAD VEACH, Lead Pastor of Zoe Church, Los Angeles

"Mike Kai's book, *That Doesn't Just Happen,* is an insightful expose of important lessons for today's society drawn from a brief but powerful Bible encounter. Pastor Mike stresses the necessity of certain values such as excellence and intentional interaction with people while drawing instances from his personal life alongside the biblical duo of King Solomon and the Queen of Sheba.

"It is a book that embodies the author's desire to help people cultivate a nurturing culture and expand their horizons within and outside the Christian community. I hope that at whatever point you have reached, this book will inspire you to do the best you can and be the best you can, right here and right now. I hope it will help us all see quality like Sheba and build greatness like Solomon. Thanks, Mike!"

—COURTNEY MCBATH, Leadership Coach/Pastor

"In *That Doesn't Just Happen,* Mike Kai offers an essential call to leaders to serve with excellence, curate a thriving culture, and be the best you can with what you have right now! If you're ready to go the extra mile in your leadership but aren't sure how to begin, this book is for you!"

—MARTIJN VAN TILBORGH, Author, speaker, and entrepreneur

"The greatest witness in the 21st century, whether in business or the Church, is having a spirit of excellence is everything you do. Excellence is the differentiator; it's attractive and draws people to take notice. In *That Doesn't Just Happen*, my great friend Mike Kai brings practical insight to timeless principles and wisdom that will help every business leader and pastor ensure what is being built will last. This timely book is your guide to moving from mediocrity to excellence."

—LEE DOMINGUE, International speaker, author, and entrepreneur

"Mike Kai is the kind of pastor that, as a businessman, I would want as my pastor! His ability to not only understand how a business person thinks, but also have the skills to speak into their lives and set them on purpose and mission is priceless. I believe this book will be a valuable tool in helping you take bigger, better, and more profitable steps forward in your business and ultimately in financing the Kingdom of God!"

—ANDREW DENTON, Kingdom builder

"The principles and concepts that Mike shares can positively accelerate everything that you touch. With skill and insight, he reveals great qualities of two ancient leaders and their kingdoms, dissecting and analyzing the importance of having a culture of excellence and how implementing works. I highly recommend this book."

—BOB HARRISON, Founder of Christian Business Leaders Intl

"*That Doesn't Just Happen* will inspire you to develop your God-given gifts in ways you've never considered. I'm blessed to mentor and to be a pastor to Mike Kai, so I know firsthand how his dynamic faith and fresh perspective can make a huge positive difference. Drawing on biblical wisdom, historical research, Mike's diverse work experience, and a contagious passion for excellence, this book will lift you to next-level leadership."

—CHRIS HODGES, Senior Pastor of Church of the Highlands and author of *The Daniel Dilemma* and *Out of the Cave*

THAT DOESN'T JUST HAPPEN

HOW
EXCELLENCE
ACCELERATES
EVERYTHING

MIKE KAI

INSPIRE

Dedication

To my mother, Esther Jimenez Kai. I am so thankful that you pushed for long family vacations even though we didn't have all the resources growing up. Our horizons were expanded when we visited national parks and big cities, yet we were blessed that you raised us in the best small town in Hawaiʻi.

To my father, John Kaleinani Kai. You took a bold risk when you changed careers in your late 30s. You have modeled hospitality and an entrepreneurial spirit, and your children received their "go-getter" mentality from you.

I love you both and am indebted to you.

Love, Mike

FOREWORD

Are there Bible stories that you identify with repeatedly? These episodes jump out at you.

David inspires the underdogs. Daniel speaks to those needing courage. Visionary leaders love Nehemiah. So why does Mike Kai gravitate toward King Solomon and the Queen of Sheba? In his introduction to this book, he sprinkles self-descriptors that explain why.

Some of those self-descriptors are inspirer, entrepreneur, curious, and learner—much like both Solomon and the Queen of Sheba.

An author writes a book because they have a burning message that they are passionate about and feel that if others grasped the message and acted on it, their lives and organizations will improve vastly.

I have known Mike Kai for many years and have observed characteristics and actions that personify this book. He named his church Inspire. He started a leadership network and called it Inspire. He started a leadership brand, including a quarterly leadership journal, and named it Inspire.

The Queen of Sheba had to be inspired enough to make the intercontinental trek to personally meet the inspirer himself.

So what is this book really all about? It's about you.

How you can be a better you. How you can serve others better. How you can organize and lead a better organization.

You can learn all that by drawing pragmatic lessons from the lives of King Solomon and The Queen of Sheba.

Mike Kai wants us to Build Like Solomon and See Like Sheba so we can finish better.

I want to; you will, too.

—SAM CHAND, Leadership Consultant and author of *Harnessing the Power of Tension*

ACKNOWLEDGMENTS

Afterter completing my second book, *Plateaus*, which was a follow-up to *The Pound for Pound Principle*, I didn't know when I would write my next. People had been asking me that very question: "When will you write your next book?" Truth be told, I honestly didn't know what I would write about next or even when. Nothing grabbed my attention enough.

I would liken writing a book to a lot like giving birth to a baby. I've never experienced it myself, but I've seen my wife go through it! Giving birth to something so important and delivering it with the highest quality was my biggest concern. But, oh, the labor pains!

So . . . here it is! Welcome to the world, *That Doesn't Just Happen*.

This book wouldn't be possible without the encouragement and support of my wife and best friend, Lisa, and our three daughters, Courtney, Rebekah, and Charis. I also want to acknowledge those who've encouraged me on this journey: Martijn van Tilborgh and Dr. Sam Chand. There are key staff members who have spent long hours on this project with me: Chelsea Robinson, Clint Chinen, D. J. Garces, Evie Carranza, Leanne Thomas, and Dr. John Brangenberg. Also, thank you to Ken Walker for understanding my writing style, keeping my voice in the book, and yet editing with excellence. I also want to thank the amazing congregation at Inspire Church, the

Influencer's Network, and the Inspire Collective. And lastly, I must give thanks to the Lord for giving me a great subject to write on that I hope inspires many!

CONTENTS

Introduction: No "Pixie Dust" Here 15

**PART 1. BUILD LIKE KING SOLOMON:
   CREATING A CULTURE OF EXCELLENCE** 20

CHAPTER 1. Excellence in The Process 21

CHAPTER 2. Excellence in The Details 41

CHAPTER 3. Excellence in The Curation 59

CHAPTER 4. Excellence in The Culture 79

**PART 2. SEE LIKE THE QUEEN OF SHEBA:
   CREATIVE ADAPTATION & CULTURAL
   CONTEXTUALIZATION** 98

CHAPTER 5. See The Hard Truths 99

CHAPTER 6. See The Potential 117

PART 3. FINISH BETTER: CULTIVATING A LEGACY 136

CHAPTER 7. Build To Change 137

CHAPTER 8. Build To Last 153

CHAPTER 9. Build To Leave A Legacy 167

CHAPTER 10. Keep Enterprising If You Want
                To Keep Rising 185

Conclusion...203

Appendix 207

INTRODUCTION
NO "PIXIE DUST" HERE

Growing up, I always had my sights set on becoming a businessman. Like many of you reading these words, I began working in my early teen years. My initial endeavors included a yard-cleaning business, a newspaper delivery route, and even a small babysitting service. (That one didn't suit me too well and quickly ended!) In my mid-teens I graduated to a steadier paycheck, working as a delivery driver in charge of my own van and routes and often driving round trips of 250 miles per day. I worked at gas stations and grocery stores, too. Up until my sophomore year of college, I was also part of the United States Air Force ROTC program, but I wound up on a different path.

Ultimately, my winding journey has led me to become a pastor, something I never planned nor expected. Yet here I am, fulfilling my purpose as the senior pastor of a large and influential church in Hawai'i. I know what you're thinking: *Hold up. Is this guy going to preach to me and pull scripture from the Bible to make his points?* Don't fret, dear reader! I promise to keep this light and not so preachy. In fact, I think you will find applications from this book that extend well beyond the church. So, if you are in business, the nonprofit world, or any other arenas that require a strong leadership and visionary role, stick with me. I got you.

Despite my current status in the church world, there is something in my background that I couldn't shake, which is the reason I wrote this book. Because that part of me always wanted to be in business, from my teenage years on, I fancied myself an entrepreneur. In my early twenties, I started a side hustle in multilevel marketing. While I later had to bow out of that arena to devote more time and attention to my calling, the silver lining behind my transition to a different season was the time I devoted to reading content related to that endeavor. It was there I learned about the authors whose books made a lasting impact on my life in the area of—wait for it—business. I read material by such motivational writers as Robert Schuller and Norman Vincent Peale, inspirational writers like Og Mandino (If you've never heard of him, you need to look him up.), and practical authors like Ken Blanchard and speaker and author Bob Harrison.

In more recent times I read a fascinating book (*Excellence Wins* released in early 2019) by Horst Schulze, the cofounder and first president of the Ritz-Carlton Hotel Company; eight years after starting Ritz-Carlton, he was named "Corporate Hotelier of the World" by an industry publication. Then, of course, I also read books by one of my heroes and mentors, bestselling author and leadership expert John Maxwell, and one of my all-time favorites and mentor, Dr. Sam Chand.

All of these people are like echoes from the past, mixing with voices in the present. They have helped shape me and influence me as an author, a speaker, a pastor, and a businessman. They share the credit for my musings in these pages, which are based upon the interaction between the Queen of Sheba and King Solomon, as chronicled in the Bible in 1 Kings and 1 Chronicles.

That Doesn't Just Happen doesn't have its origins in a lengthy series, transcribed into book format for mass consumption (even though there's nothing wrong with repurposing content). Only recently did I preach a sermon about this topic. However, as the COVID-19 crisis of 2020 stretched into many months and flared up again in the fall, I decided: *Why not do what I've always wanted to do and write a book about my passion?* Namely, to write a book about customer service, culture curating, creative adaptation, and contextual application. If I lost anyone with these terms, rest assured I'll explain more as we go.

The queen brought 120 talents of gold out of the abundance of her treasuries to Solomon. A "talent" is typically considered to be the equivalent of 75 pounds. So, 120 talents of gold would be the equivalent of 144,000 ounces of gold, or a staggering $285 million-plus by today's market values. Yet that was mere pocket change for the Queen of Sheba. But wait, there's more. She also brought with her more spices than Jerusalem had ever seen, plus precious stones! Who does that? The Queen of Sheba did. She was an unnamed queen of a mysterious country; historians have kept us wanting more information.

What we do know is what she brought and its value. Thus, we can deduce she lived in opulence and already had an established kingdom, where commerce and trade made the people great and was much of what they valued. She was surely a woman of excellence who came from South Sahara, Yemen, or Ethiopia, countries in the Arabian Peninsula and Northern Africa. If you removed modern borders and country names, it would yield a spacious region.

When it comes to King Solomon and the Queen of Sheba, we are left to only a few commentaries with too few paragraphs. We must settle for a Google search and the trails where that leads. However, we also can rely on our imagination. See, King Solomon might be the main subject, but it's the Queen of Sheba who will steal our hearts. Because "game recognizes game," royalty recognizes royalty, and regal-ness is a by-product, a common mutual respect existed between these two monarchs. But what the queen witnessed, felt, saw, and experienced was unlike anything she expected.

You want principles? We got that. You want "how to"? Yes, we do. While there are a great variety of books on the topic of customer service, excellence, and culture, I have set out to write a book that honors the queen, highlights her observations, and makes for enjoyable reading. I am also seeking to show everyone that God inspires excellence, and excellence is not brought about by a fairy's wave of the wand or pixie dust that just happens to be sprinkled on someone's life or business. I want to share with you *why* and *how* excellence can accelerate everything you touch, and in turn, the lives of other people as well.

As such, or because of the aforementioned, I have taken a bit of creative license with my narrative. This is not a theological treatise. There are plenty of great books and authors for that, but *this* book *is not that.* It was difficult to find credible sources of authentic historical contextualization about the Queen of Sheba. There are urban legends and gossipy stories about a supposed love affair between the king and queen, but I paid them no credence. I was looking at—and for—evidence on business and life principles we can take away from what King Solomon built, what the Queen of Sheba saw, and how we can avoid their pitfalls in order to finish better.

The Bible says many came to sit at Solomon's feet and learn from him. I have to believe these kingdoms sent their most intelligent, excellent men and women to learn from Solomon. I have also come to believe this was neither an ordinary visit or conference they attended nor a recommended podcast they quickly listened to and forgot about. I have to believe they took home and implemented everything they learned.

I think they learned lessons they were able to adapt to their own context and for the betterment of their kingdoms. And I believe those same lessons are found in the life of Solomon and applicable today. It is my hope that *That Doesn't Just Happen* will somehow do the same in whatever sphere of influence you lead.

God bless, and let's go!

—*Mike Kai*

part one

01: Excellence in The Process

02: Excellence in The Details

03: Excellence in The Curation

04: Excellence in The Culture

BUILD LIKE KING SOLOMON: CREATING A CULTURE OF EXCELLENCE

EXCELLENCE IN THE PROCESS

*A culture of excellence doesn't just happen.
It's intentional, and it starts with leadership.*

01

It may be a challenge to transport yourself back in time some three thousand years, but put your imagination to work. Envision yourself as part of the Queen of Sheba's camel caravan bearing gold, jewels, and expensive spices as it neared its destination: Israel. When she got to the top of Mount Zion, the queen couldn't believe what she was seeing. It was not just the higher elevation and cooler air that blew eastward from the Mediterranean Sea. Or the snow-capped mountains of Lebanon situated to the north. No, it was that she had never imagined that she would finally be looking down from this mountain at something she had heard of and now was seeing for the first time. Indeed, it was worth the three months or so that it had taken her to arrive.

It must not have been an easy trip, but it started with what she had heard about Solomon. In that long-ago day and time, neither travel nor communication flowed as easily as it does in the modern, instantaneous, always-connected era. In the ancient world, trade routes and well-worn desert highways represented treacherous journeys. The heat from the blazing sun reflecting off the hot sands could fry an egg without a magnifying glass. Plentiful numbers of marauders and bandits patrolled the highways and byways with the same merciless efficiency as their pirate counterparts on the high seas. If the heat didn't get you, the bandits might.

Since in desert climes water was always needed, a foray through the desert would mean taking the original

Yeti bottles: rough goatskins, ferried on the backs of donkeys and camels. Such a trip could mean delays from sandstorms, circling the wagons to protect against enemy threats, or servants needing attention because of extreme dehydration. The potential challenges facing a caravan plowing its way through the desert? Daunting, to say the least. Yet when word came to the Queen of Sheba that there was no greater or more magnificent city within traveling distance than Jerusalem—and no man with greater wisdom than Solomon—she paid close attention. The traveling inconveniences she might encounter were going to be worth making it to her destination. She had a clear objective to see both this promised city of unfathomable riches and to learn more about the mighty King Solomon.

Raised in royalty and doing her best to advance a kingdom and protect the realm, she was obviously intrigued. But she did not hear of Solomon's greatness just once. Over the course of months and years, she began to hear it more frequently. Finally, she thought, I must see with my own eyes what I am hearing with my two ears.

A GRAND VISIT

So, with great anticipation and the necessary planning, strategizing, and stocking of provisions to fuel the royal traveling party, the queen initiated a site visit of grand proportions. No greater wealth would ever leave the country, no greater gifts would ever be given, than what she would bestow on the legendary King of Israel about whom she had heard so much. Her plans to visit King Solomon and the Kingdom of Israel called for determining logistics, gathering supplies, and mapping out possible routes.

The entourage and military caravan led by proud soldiers at the front and another squadron at the rear, all riding on stately, decorated camels, must have caused quite a stir among onlookers in Jerusalem. Not only would the presence of so many dignitaries, servants, and soldiers cause eyes to widen but also the precious cargo they carried that symbolized the worthiness of such an escort. It wasn't just the gold, jewels, and spices that were so impressive. So was the beautiful and yet mysterious, dark-skinned woman who hailed from a southern kingdom, protected and cared for by her eunuchs and ladies-in-waiting. The procession would definitely have piqued the curiosity of a people unaccustomed to such a curious and beautiful sight.

Of course, their arrival would have been announced by an advance party. The queen would likely have dispatched a small traveling party of emissaries to smooth the road and pave the way with gifts to King Solomon and his court before her arrival. This was no ordinary visit; no protocols would be overlooked as her officials stepped down from their camels and offered their gifts after being escorted through the impressive gates of the holy city. They returned to their traveling party, excited over how well they were received and the respect and honor accorded them. *This is a promising trip*, they must have thought to themselves (to put it lightly).

The Queen of Sheba set out on a journey that would change her life forever. It would expose her court officials to excellence and the very best. In witnessing what creating a culture of excellence would do for them, it would expand their horizons, widen the queen's influence, and open her eyes to more than she had previously imagined to be possible. This journey would ultimately further prosper her country through the resulting trade agreements and protect her people by creating allies in Israel. In addition, this site visit would open her country's eyes to a God (Yahweh) who would bless her people for centuries to come. It would result in the story of the treasurer of Ethiopia being baptized by Philip in the Book of Acts (Acts 8:26–39) and land her name in the Bible, as well as in legends and stories told for hundreds of years to come. She would go up to Jerusalem one way and return another—as a different person.

There is much we can learn from her visit, since it reveals truths and principles on which we can build our own organizations as we emphasize excellence:

1. THE PRINCIPLE OF DECONSTRUCTION

Principle: Deconstructing can reveal insights you
can build upon; also known as reverse engineering.

One reason I am so intrigued with the story of Solomon and the
Queen of Sheba is my penchant for discovering new things. I
wanted to know more about this mysterious encounter of which
the biblical narrative is rather brief. Setting out to learn more
reflects my nature throughout life. I've always been fascinated
by the way things work. I was the child in the family who would
excitedly anticipate opening one gift on Christmas Eve and then
go crazy on Christmas morning opening the rest. But what differentiated me from my brothers and sister was that my most
favorite toys on Christmas morning would end up broken by
the end of the day.

The reason for this rather curious phenomenon? My ongoing
attempts to take apart my toys to see how they worked. I wanted
to see why the wheels turned a figure around, why that long
plastic stick—which looked like a whip with a T handle—had
all those plastic teeth on it, or how Kenner made that cool toy
car wind up and run. On the slightly more gruesome side, how
could I pop GI Joe's shoulder out of its socket and put it back
into place? I've always been the curious one asking questions

like, "How does it work?" . . . "Why does it work that way?" . . . "Is there a better way to do this?"

I would say I am a builder by training and a deconstructor by nature. I can build things like businesses and buildings, but I also immediately begin to pick things apart. I want to know how it works and sometimes more importantly, why things did not work. Such as: where was the communication breakdown, where did we drop the ball, and how can we prevent that from happening again? Yet, despite this inveterate curiosity about toys, rarely could I determine how to put any of them back together again. Humpty Dumpty would definitely not have wanted me on his team!

Still, leadership requires us to become deconstructionists. That is much different from being someone who likes to demolish things in *Wreck-It Ralph* style. What separates an excellent leader from an average leader is that the latter figures out why their systems and structures are not working and improves them. For example, in recent times, the deconstruction of cuisine has taken off as a trend. Chefs have studied other chefs' culinary creations, deciphered what the core ingredients and ideas are, and dismantled the food down to its basic components. Then, unconventionally serving in creative ways, these newer chefs have discovered different ways to apply this creative adaption while adding their own flair to the dish. And, they charge an extra twenty dollars for it!

Despite my limited mechanical abilities, I believe the curiosity and intrigue behind my young mind has carried on through to today. I keep asking the same kinds of questions I did as an eight year old. Just add a few more decades to life, and some things never change. That's what prompted me to write a book on Solomon and the Queen of Sheba and the story's inherent applications to creating a culture, curating it, and creatively adapting it into other contexts.

For instance, much can be learned about quality, excellence, and customer service just by going to a five-star restaurant for dinner. While this dining experience may last for an hour and a half, customer service and excellence start way before you enter the establishment (more about that later).

Now, at the risk of sounding like a fossil, I was raised in a day and age where we were taught to respect our elders and that—whether at a restaurant, in a retail store, or running a simple lawn mowing business—the customer was always right. In a fast-paced, selfie generation raised on a diet of social media, I feel we've lost a lot of that ethic. However, I also feel that the lost art of customer service and excellence can be recaptured and applied to a younger generation that is more tech-savvy, app-literate, and globally connected than anyone over the age of 50 could ever have imagined.

Still, there's something missing behind a smartphone, a Google search, and an OpenTable app. "What's missing?" you ask. A desire to honor our guests. On a personal level, we demonstrate this by deep-cleaning our homes before out-of-town guests arrive. Having fresh towels, sheets, and even basic toiletries available demonstrates to our guests that we are happy to see them and honored by their presence. This is the kind of excellence that distinguishes the Ritz-Carlton from the average hotel. When people bring this kind of outlook, service, and performance to daily life and make it part of their journey, it enriches others' lives, satisfies customers and clients, and expands the business.

2. INTENTIONALITY SHAPES EXPERIENCE

Principle: Intentional leadership is required
to shape the experiences you desire.

Applying this principle to a church context, we've intentionally shaped our weekend service environments, social media strategies, online events, and outreaches to expand the impact that Inspire Church is making in hundreds of thousands of lives—locally and globally. One of the most important shifts we have focused on is our "connect groups." These home-based groups meet weekly, following the model of discipleship outlined in the New Testament: teaching, fellowship, breaking of bread, praising God, and prayer. During the 2020 season of shutdowns, we moved all our groups online. It was a radical but necessary change to increase and strengthen people's faith.

However, newcomers aren't necessarily going to feel comfortable sitting down at someone's home for a connect group right away. That normally takes a bit of time, and COVID-19 conditions have changed a lot of people's comfort levels. That's why as we grew from a church of a few dozen two decades ago to where we are now, we decided to create a culture that would prove attractive to those outside the church and pave the way for them to explore a relationship with Jesus.

In our first two years after launching, I learned very quickly about creating the type of environment in which the right type of culture would grow our church. We wanted something that grew deep and wide. In the beginning and for the first seven years or so, our growth was steady, healthy, and incremental. Of course, it wasn't fast enough for me personally, but it was growing! The key was that the culture wasn't accidental or created by default. It was intentional and on purpose.

Although growth was incremental at first, as we began to move up and to the right of the chart and then mushroomed beyond that, we realized we had a bit of a tiger by the tail. It quickly became apparent that I needed to know who was doing what and how well they were doing that job. As senior pastor, I had to have a more efficient way of knowing we were managing this hockey-stick growth rate. Some management consultants would call these your KPIs: Key Performance Indicators. We called them our metrics. Whatever they're called, they are critical, because the old saying is true: What you measure grows and what you neglect grows.

Fast forward to today. When the early 2020 shutdowns happened and our state issued a shelter-in-place order, I quickly pivoted the church to embrace these new realities. We were encouraged as our viewership numbers skyrocketed beyond our expectations! I was encouraged to teach on and about how we functioned locally and globally as Inspire Church. Recently we discussed culture to inform all the newcomers and the mushrooming online audience we welcomed during the pandemic what we were all about. We needed to tell them: "This is how we do it here; this is the culture of Inspire."

So, in the middle of 2020, while I was still doing primarily pre-recorded sermons, this is what I told them: "If you were going to come to Hawai'i and came to our parking lot at the Waikele shopping center, I bet that by the time you pulled in, you'd have 'chicken skin.' You'd be thinking to yourself, *Wow, there's something about this place that just feels different.*

"When you got out of your car and walked up to the front, naturally you'd feel a little nervous. But you'd also feel this sense of welcome. When you walked through the doors, you'd see the different kinds of people who are a part of this congregation. People from many different races, ethnicities, ages—you name it.

"And then you'd walk in and you'd see the building and hopefully you would realize, *Wow, this is really nice. This is an incredible lobby—there's a cross in the lobby, how amazing.* And then you would see the sign that says, 'Welcome Home.' Then the deeper you came into this place, you'd think, *Wow, look at all this technology . . . this is pretty amazing.* Then you would see the worship team and hear the pulsing music and worship with us. You'd feel the presence of God in this place. There would be a part of you that wants to cry and a part of you that doesn't want to let go. You know what I'm talking about? And then you'd think, *WOW! This must happen every-where!* But the truth of the matter is this: No, *this* does not 'just happen.' It is *intentional.*"

A culture of excellence doesn't just happen. It's intentional, and it starts with leadership. The team at the top must establish the tone, set the example, plan the execution, and then trust those they have trained to carry out the mission. This is true for every business and organization and is important for every customer, congregant, and client.

3. WHEN "GOOD ENOUGH" IS THE ENEMY
OF EXCELLENCE

Principle: Excellent service requires
going beyond what's normal.

In the introduction, I mentioned my teenage forays into a series of entrepreneurial endeavors and regular employment. I didn't chronicle my service in the airline industry, which began at the age of nineteen and continued (with other part-time work along the way) for twelve years. You could say I worked in the "back of the house," since hardly any travelers saw us baggage handlers and cabin cleaners as we toiled day by day. When I started as an inexperienced young man, I was the youngest employee on the ramp for American Airlines (AA) at Honolulu International Airport.

I learned some bad habits along the way, such as what "good enough" looked like. I should note that delivering this kind of performance meant you wouldn't last long, nor would fellow employees who took pride in their work allow you to get away with it. During my twelve years of employment with American, the great CEO Robert Crandall led the company. His innovation with the SABRE computer reservation system revolutionized airline travel. Along with the airline industry's first-of-its-kind miles reward program (called AAdvantage Miles), Crandall's leadership thrust AA to the top. It eventually acquired such airlines as TWA and Air Cal and, in particular, their routes. Once a winner of the prestigious Horatio Alger Award, Crandall would see his innovations copied by others across the airline and travel industry, forever changing global travel.

There are eight hotels named after King Solomon in parts of the world like Israel, Nigeria, the Solomon Islands, the United Kingdom, the Philippines, and Ghana, and a landmark located in Australia. Similarly, you can find four Queen of Sheba hotels located throughout Israel, Ethiopia, and Tanzania.

I also learned from managers what excellent customer service looks like. They taught me how to load a bag properly, including putting it in the right baggage compartment in order for that luggage to make its way across the Pacific Ocean and through several different stops. These steps ensured when the customer arrived at the other end of their trip and went to the baggage claim carousel, they indeed received their luggage, and saved them from the nightmare of waiting a day for their necessities to arrive. (Anyone who has waited in line at midnight to file a missing luggage claim after several flight delays en route can appreciate that kind of service.)

I also learned what it means to provide sparkling clean toilets on the plane, replacing used pillowcases with fresh ones, organizing the seat pocket material, wiping down trays, and not allowing a single crumb to be seen on the seats or floors that were my responsibility. I learned how to work with the in-flight crew, captains, and stewardesses, and relate to those hardworking staff members who were working face-to-face with customers. I learned that many of those customers had embraced a lifelong dream to come to Hawai'i. Consequently, we did not want to taint a single moment of the beauty of this place and the hospitality of its people.

While not everything was under our control, there was much that we could control when we were highly responsible for every hardworking, high-paying customer. In addition to those details we could pay attention to, there were others that were beyond our capability to control, such as flight delays in other venues that affected our arrivals and departures. And there was also one beautiful thing that we couldn't control: the gorgeous Hawai'i weather.

I've heard it said that many people save all their lives to come to this beautiful spot in the middle of the Pacific Ocean. On their arrival from such destinations in the heartland as Des Moines, Iowa; Nashville, Tennessee; Fargo, North Dakota; or

Midland-Odessa, Texas, I observed passengers as they unbuckled their seatbelts, retrieved their luggage from the overhead compartment, and stepped onto the jet bridge. Smiles would cross their faces as the gorgeous scenery, pleasant warmth and atmosphere, and the smell of plumeria flowers (a tantalizing mix of such scents as honeysuckle, citrus, and peach) let people know: "You're not in Kansas anymore, Toto." I didn't want to ruin anyone's dream vacation.

4. THE IMPORTANCE OF AN EXCELLENT EDUCATION

Principle: Challenging seasons instill
great lessons for high standards.

By the time I was twenty-one years old, I'd become a single father, raising my then two-year-old daughter, Courtney. As her sole provider, I needed to grow up fast. Needless to say, it was one of the most difficult times of my life. I had no choice but to discontinue my college education at the University of Hawai'i. I took on two part-time jobs (to equal the pay of full-time employment) in order to provide for Courtney and survive. Along with my hopes of entering the US Air Force as a second lieutenant after completing my degree, other dreams flew out the window.

Survival mode was in full effect, and let me tell you, the struggle was real! Unbeknownst to me, I had automatically enrolled in the College of Hard Knocks, and would go to graduate with a master's degree from the University of Success. ("Siri, play *There Goes My Life* by Kenny Chesney.")

As if I weren't busy enough, I signed on with a multilevel marketing (MLM) business. It was during this phase I learned to grind, made presentations, read amazing books, and attended numerous master-mind groups. I stuck with it for five years. There is no doubt this phase was part of the setback that was needed to set up my next growth phase. The MLM grind was a necessary detour I needed to get my mind right for what was yet to come. This was also when I began going to church regularly. That's where I learned about God's love for me and where I decided to surrender and dedicate my life to Jesus. All this by the age of twenty-one!

So, let's recap: a single dad raising a two-year-old girl dedicates his life to God, has no college degree—but two great part-time jobs; add in a MLM business, mix it all up, and what you get is a recipe for . . . whatever you want it to be.

The second job in my journey through my twenties was at The Willows, a well-known historical restaurant set in a gorgeous emerald garden in suburban Honolulu that takes one's breath away.

The Willows stood in the midst of a beautiful three-acre parcel of land. A local landmark, it was a favorite spot for celebrating birthdays, weddings, and other milestones. Owned by the late Randy Lee, over the eight years I worked there I gathered many insights about customer service, hospitality, direction, and humility. I started as a busboy, then became a member of the banquet staff, and finally worked as a valet. My education in customer service was a hard-earned, hard-learned one, but this experience gave me an eye for excellence (which can be considered a blessing or a curse). Sometimes I can't even relax when I'm on vacation because I can see all the things that *could be* better. It's not that I harbor a critical spirit—but that I have developed a discerning eye.

Mr. Lee helped me develop this discernment. He was a true gentleman who drove a tasteful Jaguar and often wore shining white shoes to match his white slacks. He also liked to wear a classy Hawaiian shirt—not some cheap imitation you can find at a swap meet or the cheesy ones that college students wear with fake plastic leis around their necks and sunblock on their noses as they party like it's 1999. ("Siri, play *1999* by Prince.") Nope. Mr. Lee always wore a one-of-a-kind, designer-made creation. He also wore a nice gold watch or a silver one, depending on the occasion. And, a black Onyx ring with gold for his wedding band. I rarely heard him raise his voice because he didn't have to—his chefs did it for him!

The most amazing of these chefs was a woman named Kusuma Kooray, who was born and raised in Sri Lanka; her husband was a professor at the University of Hawai'i. Let me assure you, she knew how to run a kitchen with an iron fist. I would say she was the original Iron Chef! However, within a few months I was able to win her soft heart. She loved me because of my innate curiosity and hard work. Later, I will tell you more about my experience at The Willows, which made such an impression on me in those early years. At the time, I was too young and too preoccupied to realize what a great treasure it was to work for Mr. Lee and Kusuma (as we called her).

My experiences at American Airlines and those at The Willows, coupled with a mind eager to learn how things work, have instilled in me a desire to help people do the best they can with what they have—not what they wish they had—utilizing the gifts, talents, abilities, and know-how that are part of their intrinsic make-up. *That Doesn't Just Happen* is giving me the opportunity to fulfill that mission.

It doesn't matter if you are in the hotel industry, a restaurateur, the manager of a nonprofit, or a business executive. You could be older but young at heart, or you could be younger and just a few lessons away from an incredible career. My hope is that at whatever point you have reached, this book will inspire you to do the best you can and be the best you can—right here and right now. I hope it will help you to build like Solomon as you see like the Queen of Sheba in your quest for excellence.

EXCELLENCE IN THE DETAILS

In my experience, when people know and feel you have their best interests at heart, they will do anything—if the cause is big enough and they know you truly care.

02

One of the first lessons I learned from my hardworking parents is that if you're going to do something, always do it well and finish what you started. If you're going to perform shoddy work or do something in a half-hearted manner, then you are doing others and yourself a disservice. Years later, I can still hear Mom's voice calling, "Do it right or don't do it at all." My mother wasn't being mean; she was helping me for a lifetime.

King David had the same kind of parental concern for Solomon. David cared about his country and wanted to set up his son to succeed. But David had a heavy burden on his heart. He felt strongly Israel needed a central place of worship: a place that would honor God with excellence. So, David pulled all his resources together and called in favors from all of the contacts he had made over the years. One of the biggest supporters of this unprecedented building project would be Tyre's King Hiram—the supplier of some of the finest wood to build the temple in Jerusalem. David would import other fine materials, but he also stockpiled gold, silver, bronze, the finest carved limestone blocks, ivory, and textiles.

Following David's death, Solomon received an unusual dream. In it, God asked him to pick anything he wanted. While Solomon could ask for anything as the new king of Israel, he asked for wisdom. God told Solomon he could have asked for peace on his borders and with his enemies, and He would have granted it.

Solomon could have asked for a long life, but he didn't. Solomon could have requested untold riches, but he asked for wisdom to lead the people of Israel because the task was far beyond his capacity and experience. So as a gift, God gave him everything he didn't request. Solomon would enjoy a long life, untold riches, peace with his enemies—and wisdom to boot! That was how Solomon became the wisest king who ever lived, with a national economy, unparalleled in his time and even after his reign ended.

DESIGNER OF EXCELLENCE

Two of the most influential designers of the twentieth century were Charles Eames and his wife, Ray. The longtime partners rose to fame in the post-World War II years after opening a studio in the chic Los Angeles suburb of Venice. One accomplishment on a lengthy list took place during the war: They adapted a plywood molding technique developed for furniture design to create emergency splints for injured soldiers. "We don't do 'art'—we solve problems," Charles said of this creation. "How do we get from where we are to where we want to be?"[1]

That their influence is still alive long after Charles died in 1978, and Ray a decade later, is a testament to their skills, vision, persistence, and determination. In recent years, such prestigious publications as *The Atlantic* carried stories about them. So did the BBC, which ran a feature in 2017 in conjunction with the opening of a new exhibition of their work at the Vitra Design Museum in Weil am Rhein, Germany. The BBC noted that while they were most famous for the iconic chairs that transformed ideas of modern furniture, they were also graphic and textile designers, architects, and filmmakers, with 125 shorts to their credit. Commented journalist William Cook: "If they'd confined their efforts to just one of these genres, we'd still be talking about them today. Yet they spread their talents far and wide . . ."[2]

The buildings they designed were considered some of the greatest structures built in the 1970s. Charles and Ray—he the visionary, she the one who paid attention to details—inspired other architects to achieve their very best. This was not only in the way a building functioned and appeared, but also in the ways in which it encouraged people to interact in the workplace. In designing their award-winning homes, they encouraged the idea that allowed one living space to flow into another. This gave families enough privacy while keeping them in quick contact with one another when so desired. That these creative geniuses paid such painstaking attention to detail meant they produced an "unparalleled breadth of creative design work across many disciplines."[3] In fact, the Eameses' furniture design, architecture, and incredible ability to collaborate with their team came from their philosophy that the details are not the details; they are the design. This dynamic duo were people after Solomon's own heart.

DETAILS, SCHMETAILS

Details are important. Ask anyone who has been audited by the Internal Revenue Service! Ask anyone who has been to traffic court because they forgot about those pesky parking tickets. Ask any roommate in charge of the food bills and the receipts, and they will tell you: Without providing the details to others, they don't get paid back.

By the time the Queen of Sheba arrived in Jerusalem, Solomon and his staff had mastered the details—not only the details of a magnificent scope of exterior building design, and interior quality and excellence, but also of attention to details in the way their team operated. You can bet Solomon and his supervisors worked on coaching the workers about such things as the expression on their faces. ("You should all look happy to be here. There are thousands of Hebrews who would love to have your position!")

Remember, in those days kings—not just Solomon, but kings all over the world—were all-powerful figures, due homage and respect. Imagine if any one of their staff rolled their eyes or sighed loudly out of frustration over a request and what kind of dressing-down they'd get later. It wouldn't be pretty. But the point here isn't that kings and those in authority had the ability to lop off one's head. It was the coaching and standards they set for those in their employ that made such a difference in the excellence their employees exhibited.

Those fortunate to be working at the palace would have been coached on their posture ("Stand up straight and pull your shoulders back!"), when they should make eye contact with guests, or when they should gaze into the distance, as if they hadn't seen anything or heard comments they were not supposed to repeat. Additionally, their ability to solve problems with wisdom (I'm sure the wisdom thing rubbed off on Solomon's people.) and speed in arriving at creative solutions was something that must have been drilled into them. Such attention to details shows you actually *care about what you do*, *who you are serving* (the customer), and *who you do it with*.

CONSCIOUS CARING

There are bedrock principles behind caring for others and how we carry out the tasks we have been given:

1. CARE ABOUT WHAT YOU DO

Principle: Pay attention to the details.

First, let's talk about *caring about what you do*. When you care about the details of your uniform, how you are groomed, and how you present yourself to customers, it shows you care about what you do. When you show up for work looking like you just rolled out of bed, or are dressed in the same casual sweats you wear to saunter down to the corner market, it speaks volumes.

Many people say: "Don't judge a book by its cover." Generally, I agree with that old adage. However, when it comes to business, people do judge by appearance.

It isn't just clothing that makes a difference, though. When I started as a busboy at The Willows, I arrived with experience gained in working at two well-known chain restaurants. Their philosophy could be expressed through the phrase familiar to all the busboys (and girls) who worked there: "Turn and burn." We bussed those tables in a flurry to allow those waiting outside the doors to get in, so the wait staff could carb-load them into lethargy.

Trivia Tidbits

You can still visit Aksum, Ethiopia, today to see what is believed to be the home of the Queen of Sheba and what some claim as the final resting place of the legendary Ark of the Covenant.

Now, at The Willows, supervisors wanted us to turn (bus) the tables quickly. At the same time, they wanted us to remember this restaurant had an old Hawai'i charm to it, which meant we needed to avoid the appearance of hustling customers out the door. The Willows not only was a source of affection for Honolulu residents, tourists loved it even more since they never imagined such a scenic oasis would be tucked into an urban setting.

Because it wasn't a national franchise but family-owned and operated, The Willows featured genuine Hawaiian culture and the refined atmosphere of a bygone era. Entertainers famous in Hawai'i, like pop singer Don Ho and composer Irmgard Aluli—who wrote more than 200 songs—came to play music there. Famous people were often spotted there, too: rock musician Carlos Santana; *Dirty Dancing* star Jennifer Grey; one of the greatest surfers from South Africa, champion Shaun Thompson;

pastor and motivational speaker, the late Rev. Dr. Robert Schuller; and members of the Duke University and Arizona University basketball teams.

AN EXCELLENT ATMOSPHERE

That word *atmosphere* exemplified The Willows' charm. Built over a natural spring, the Hawaiian-style restaurant opened its doors on July 4, 1944, and except for a six-year hiatus, continued serving guests until New Year's Eve of 2019. Over the years it became famous for its ambience. That included strolling musicians, open-air dining under thatched roofs, colorful koi ponds, and waiters and maître d's who wore lei's (real, not plastic; a lei is a symbol of love, friendship, and celebration). Some of the island's grandest luaus were held there.

While it was a great time, life wasn't a party for the staff. With five separate dining areas spread over three acres, we felt like marathon runners covering the distances to the kitchen and back. What made an impression on me was how much *aloha* we demonstrated for customers. The Willows became world-renowned for its homemade mango chutney, sky high banana cream pies, and distinctive Sri Lankan curry, a sign of love embodied in the "aloha" greeting. For guests, the latter represented attention to the finest detail. I would call it vital to the organization's success until 1993, when The Willows fell on hard times and closed for six years when another owner acquired it.

Despite the setback, this famed restaurant's story revolved around caring about what you do. If you don't have care for what you do and the people you do it for and with, then it's either time for a motivational pep talk with yourself, or to find another place to do that in.

If you ever get a chance to visit the nearly century-old Pike Place Fish Market in Seattle, you undoubtedly will come upon the "Fish Guys," as they call themselves. They are world famous for their fish and even more so for their customer service. Several books have been written about their philosophy and their methods; a business-oriented book about them has sold more than 1.4 million copies. They will literally throw a salmon at you and invite you to catch it. One of their most famous lines— "Love the people first: sell the fish second."—encapsulates a great principle. That same idea is captured in a comment from my friend and leadership expert John Maxwell, who says that people don't care about what you know until they know how much you care. Loving people is predicated on caring about what you do. It's a detail that you cannot afford to escape.

We live in a day and age where Yelp reviews and how many stars you receive have a huge impact on business. In today's always-on, always-connected era, everybody has the capability to be a food critic, a movie critic, or a hotel critic. Today's reality underscores the old adage: "The pen is mightier than the sword." And let's face it—we've all gone to establishments where hardly anyone makes eye contact. No smiles and no warmth coming across the countertop to welcome you to their business. I'm sure we've all felt ignored or possibly even avoided.

In business, this kind of behavior is a cardinal sin. It simply cannot happen. As soon as people walk through the door, they need to be greeted. If it's a clothing store, they don't want to be hovered over, just asked if they need any assistance. Then salespeople need to give them room and space. But ignoring them completely? The worst thing that can happen is having an employee who is indifferent to customers' needs. Not only does such indifference bleed onto other team members, it can spread like a fungus throughout the organization. It's a detail that we cannot afford to miss.

2. CARE ABOUT WHOM YOU DO IT FOR

Principle: It's all about the customers.

This is why paying attention to details is critical. Not just caring about what you do, but *about whom you do it for*. Because at the end of the day, it's all about the customer. If you have no customers, you have no business. No business means no new business, new customers, and no profits. Without profits, a business will not stay afloat. So you could have great food and ambiance and pay hundreds of thousands (if not millions) of dollars to upgrade your facilities and still miss the point: Your most important assets are the people who are running the business and those who are making most of the contact with customers. We have to care about the people that we are doing it for.

"How?" you might ask. Very simple. Ask questions like, "How is your day going? Are you doing anything special on your vacation? What are you doing this weekend? How are you enjoying the holiday?" Get to know people and ask them questions that will get them talking and possibly even smiling. You will have better than decent reviews, and people will come back not only because of what you sold them, but because of how you made them feel.

From 1995 to 2014, U.S. Airways consistently ranked below average in the American Customer Satisfaction Index Score for domestic airlines. In the early 2000s, U.S. Airways—prompted by a massive customer service budget cut—decided to outsource many customer service functions. To say that was a mistaken notion would be to understate the obvious. The spike in passenger complaints and angered travelers marked the beginning of the end.

By June of 2007, a Consumer Reports *customer satisfaction survey of nearly 23,000 readers ranked U.S. Airways dead last among airlines. In April of 2008, U.S. Airways also polled last among airlines in the University of Michigan's annual American Customer Satisfaction Index. Things didn't improve over the next five years. In J.D. Power & Associates' 2013 North America Airline Satisfaction*

Study? You guessed it. Last. That year the airline began merger proceedings, with American Airlines, which were finalized in 2015.

Needless to say, the inability of U.S. Airways to address customer service problems led to its eventual demise. But this is a cautionary tale in which application goes well beyond the airline industry. The same year the U.S. Airways-American merger began, shoe giant TOMS outsourced its customer service. The results: plunging employee morale, diminished trust in the company, and cynical reactions from customers originally attracted to TOMS because of its socially conscious practices. Years later, reflecting on the situation, former executive Jake Strom commented, "Every customer interaction is a precious opportunity to grow your tribe. Saving pennies today may destroy your purpose-driven business. Movements cannot be outsourced!"[4]

3. CARE ABOUT WHOM YOU DO IT WITH

Principle: Relationships help build a culture.

The third critical detail is *whom you do it with*. This is a vital component of building a culture of excellence. As you will soon read, the Queen of Sheba gushed about the culture. Not only what she saw, but also how it made her feel. Things were articulated in such a way they will resonate for all time. We operate in a day where I believe people are often led by their feelings; what they feel and experience matters more than it did in the past. That also matters when it comes to how we relate to people we work with, work for, and lead. People need to care and know how much their leaders care.

In order to build a culture of excellence, our staff and teams must not feel it's all about the bottom line and profits. They must know they are loved, valued, cared for, and appreciated. People are not just the means to an end, even though they will help you get there. In my experience, when people know and feel you have their best interests at heart, they will do anything—if the cause is big enough and they know you truly care.

Sir H. Rider Haggard wrote King Solomon's Mines *in 1885, a fictional adventure tale loosely based on the Kingdom of Solomon, which pioneered a new literary genre known as "The Lost World."*

Now, I'm the first to admit we haven't always been the best in this department. There have been times where I'm sure we have failed staff and employees, with some feeling as though we didn't care enough about their situation. To that I say, "Fair enough." But for the majority, I'm sure their experience with us has been a great one. When staff members have felt that a new season or transition was coming in their lives, they've always given us the privilege and the honor of processing with them what their next season will look like. We've always wanted "God's best" for them. If that meant doing something else, somewhere else, then it would be good for us as well.

LOADING THE BUS

In the introduction, I mentioned reading Horst Schulze's fascinating book, *Excellence Wins*. It is full of culture of excellence gems:

- » "An organization can't please every human being every time. But it never hurts to try."
- » "Orientation must never become routine—a chore to be endured, a box to be checked off. It is crucial for establishing the platform on which all future success can be built."
- » "Elegance without warmth is arrogance."
- » "When we identify an operational function and then go looking for a warm body to fill that function, we are being short-sighted. We're treating people as just another category of things."[5]

However, what I especially appreciated were his comments on the hiring process. Like this one: "Don't hire at all. Instead, select—and then inspire."[6] Schulze's own experience bears out the wisdom of this approach. His inspiration to enter the hotel industry came during his teenage years, when he encountered "a wise maître d' who treated me and the rest of his young staff as human beings, not just function fillers." Schulze says he "will never forget him also taking time to inspire us with the mystique of the hospitality industry."[7]

One of the famed hotelier's comments particularly stuck with me: "Hire long, fire fast." Hiring and interviewing should not be a quick process. You cannot look for warm bodies or people to fog up a mirror or—so to speak—people that you have to check for a pulse. You want to hire slow and find people who fit the profile of the position, not the other way around. Then you want people who have the ability to carry out your values as an organization because they are the ones who are going to live it and uphold it.

However, it's not only about hiring the right people. As author Jim Collins says in his bestselling book, *Good to Great*, taking a company from good to great means not just getting the right people on the bus, but getting them in the right seats and teaching them what to do once they are there. So, the onboarding process of culture acclimatization should not be delegated to a fellow staff member or employee, so they can show the new person "the ropes." What they may be passing on could be detrimental to the organization's goals. As Schulze points out, the

CEO, business owner, or senior pastor should be the one leading these orientation sessions. In the past, I was guilty of too often handing this duty off to others because I rationalized that I did not have time. That is no longer the case.

Another way of making sure you have the right people on board, and that you're doing it with the right people who enjoy doing it, is constantly reinforcing your values. For us, every Tuesday through Friday morning we have something akin to a pep talk at 9:00 a.m. While it only lasts for about ten minutes, it usually has to do with reviewing one of our core values. That talk will use a biblical passage or sometimes an inspirational thought or a story, but it's all done to develop an esprit de corps among team members and staff. In other words, to have a strong team, you have to create a team spirit.

SCOUTING AN ADVENTURE

Now, I want you to put yourself in the frame of mind of someone who is scouting out an adventure, making a site visit to evaluate the reports that have filtered into your office. I want you to think about a corporate visit. Say you've heard about this incredible chain and have heard you can possibly meet the owner of Chick-fil-A, In-N-Out Burger, or Delta Airlines. You want to take your company—what you want to be—and see if the leaders of these corporate success stories can help transform your vision. So you hop on a flight and jet to their headquarters because you want to inspect firsthand what these people are doing.

This is essentially what was going on when the Queen of Sheba went to visit Solomon. The overriding question in her mind was, *How do you do what you do? Because whatever you're doing, we want to do it in our city.* With this question burning in the forefront of her consciousness, her expectations began to rise as the queen's caravan drew nearer to Jerusalem. She wasn't just feeling the change of climate from the desert to the cooler temperatures of the mountains, it was a climatization of her senses. Naturally, at higher elevations the heart rate increases to pump more blood through the system. But the Queen of Sheba's heart was beating faster because of the anticipation of what she was about to encounter.

EXCELLENCE IN THE CURATION
Behind every great team is a culture that is articulated, expressed, and taught.

03

A s the Queen of Sheba's caravan crossed the mountainous terrain, servants remarked about the crisp air. The cool breezes offered soothing relief from the stifling humidity rising from the Red Sea along the King's Highway—the customary trade route from the southern tip of Arabia to Jerusalem.

The route stretched north from Ur along the Persian Gulf to Babylon, Ashur, and Nineveh, and west to Haran and Carchemish. It ran south to Damascus and along the Transjordan (East Bank) then proceeded all the way to the tip of Arabia (modern Yemen). Various side routes branched off into Turkey, Phoenicia, Israel, Egypt, and the Red Sea. Dating back to at least 3500 B.C. and the

beginning of urban civilization, the King's Highway kept a steady flow of commerce, information, trade, and travelers moving to and through Israel and throughout the Middle East between Asia, Europe, and Africa.

As she rode into Jerusalem, the queen had great expectations of what her visit would bring, although she did not know exactly what to expect. She had heard reports of the grandeur of the First Temple, the magnificence of the palace Solomon had built, and the legendary reports that Israel's king was the wisest man who ever lived. She intended to ask him some of the questions she had mulled over since childhood, the kind of questions that had stumped even the soothsayers and scholarly advisors in the court of her mother, the Queen of the South. "Oh, Princess," they would say in condescending tones, "when you get older it will all make sense to you. Now, run along and do not concern yourself with such matters."

As she finalized her ascent on Mount Zion overlooking the city and enjoyed a view she had only imagined weeks before, the queen sat atop her camel in a state of awe and wonder. She had never seen anything like it, nor would she ever again. But she had questions on her mind and wondered in her heart if she would be granted an audience with the wisest king on the earth. She had traveled so far, and now her heart beat a little faster and her breaths came in shorter bursts. Was it the change in elevation or merely the excitement of drawing near to her destination? She wasn't sure, for never in her life had she felt such tingles running up her spine.

CULTURE: DETAILS DEFINED
(CAUGHT BUT TAUGHT)

When Solomon received the enormous task of leading a country, God also gave him the wisdom this job would require. Solomon's task would include, on a macro level, strengthening his army, enduring peace throughout the kingdom, and governing righteously. He would undoubtedly broker treaties with friendly nations and continue cultivating great relationships with other kings that his father, David, had previously established. Foremost among them was an alliance with King Hiram of Tyre (situated in modern-day Lebanon), just north of Israel.

Solomon became king of Israel at the relatively tender age of twenty. With seven years required to build the temple and thirteen to complete his palace, it is safe to say Solomon was at least forty years old by the time these two most important structures were done and dusted. He oversaw two huge building projects! This is incredible, considering his youth when they began. However, we have to remember he had divine favor and guidance over his tasks. God was working in him, through him, and with him to complete the most important and significant structure that Judaism would ever know. Yahweh Himself would live in the Holy of Holies. The Ark of the Covenant would be there, too. Not since Moses built the tabernacle in the desert during Israel's forty years of wandering had this happened.

But at the same time, Solomon helped establish another feature of life in Israel. As the foundations of the temple were set in place and everything necessary to worship there was assembled,

Solomon built two different things that would feed off each other, even though one would be greater. The first was the religious culture, with the priests leading worship and related practices. The second, which took the Queen of Sheba's breath away, was the culture of excellence.

CREATING CULTURE: THE SECRET INGREDIENT TO EVERY WINNING TEAM

People come from around the world to experience Hawai'i. While there are many beautiful places, I often think God placed His special favor on our state. On the day of creation, I can imagine Him saying, "Want to see something amazing?" And voila: Hawai'i! The Bahamas, Maldives, U.S. Virgin Islands, Tahiti, Alcatraz—they ain't got nothin' on us.

It isn't just the white sandy beaches, the crystal-blue surf of the North Shore, Kauai's lush vegetation, or the Big Island's volcanoes. There is the fascinating island culture, a concoction of genuineness, warmth, and hospitality. We can't help it; it's part of our DNA.

This innate appreciation for culture factored into my leadership when I started the church where I have been for nearly two decades now. My wife, Lisa, and I served under a very entrepreneurial pastor—I for seven years and Lisa for twelve. When he sent us out, and we launched what we would eventually brand as Inspire Church, I recognized the enormous benefits of having served in an identifiable culture. While I knew

I wanted a similar positive environment at our new church, it took a while to work out the kinks. Let me tell you . . . kinks is putting it nicely!

Still, it was definitely something I could work with. This rather modest-sized congregation had not shown any growth for thirteen years. By the time I took over the helm, they had lived through five changes of senior leadership. After ingesting a new "vision statement" every two years or so, it was all very confusing for them when I arrived. In their defense, they had legitimate reasons for wondering how long I would last.

Definition is key here: Culture is the underlying, overarching environment that shapes mores and values, which in turn determine its success. This heavily influences your success ratio, whether in a family, on a sports team, or with other groups of people.

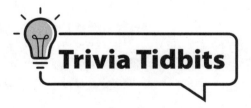

Halle Berry stars in the 1995 film, Solomon & Sheba.

As an athlete myself, I especially relate to sports metaphors and examples which is why I must confess to something I did during the pandemic that flared in 2020. I'm willing to admit that I am one of millions of people who ended up watching more than my share of Netflix during

COVID-19. I am not ashamed that since ESPN released The Last Dance—*the story about the Chicago Bulls and Michael Jordan's rise to basketball dominance—a month after widespread lockdowns began, that Lisa has caught me repeatedly watching the series. I've likely watched all ten episodes a combined nine or ten times.*

I can't help myself. First, I have been a huge Michael Jordan fan ever since he played at the University of North Carolina under the legendary coach, Dean Smith. Second, what I can't get over is the storyline and Chicago's culture of winning. It was incredible enough, but there was another element that fascinated me. Namely, the interaction between Michael Jordan and his teammates represented a culture within a culture. As one of the most recognizable people in the world at the time, "23" was on a par with Michael Jackson and Princess Diana and dominated marketing because of his brand and shoes. Yet it was the culture-within-a-culture story that kept me glued to the series. As of the writing of these words, I'm still watching.

In some ways, such a phenomenon can be detrimental. Think about it: a culture within a culture. How one reacts to its presence ultimately depends on whether it is a positive and uplifting experience, or if it exists primarily because of fear and intimidation. The duality or duplicity can send an incongruent message.

For example, say you're in the hotel business and have great facilities, five-star accommodations, and great customer service on the outside. On the inside, it's a different story, with squabbles, backbiting, jealousy, gossip, and dysfunctional personal relationships brewing. This sends the wrong message to the staff and organization. Indeed, the toxicity will eventually bleed out into your business and organization. For the Chicago Bulls, this eventually played out in public. While Coach Phil Jackson did his best to hold everything together, the team gradually dissolved. The Bulls traded away some players, didn't renew the contracts of others, and allowed Jordan—may I say the greatest basketball player of all time?—to walk away and finish his last two years of competition with the Washington Wizards. That was a sad day. You can win championships but still lose it all in the end.

DIRECTION BY DEFAULT

No matter what kind of organization you lead, a central truth is this: Either you will create the kind of culture you want, or—by default—it will be created for you. Whether a business, a nonprofit, a church, or other organization, without leadership setting the pace in creating a culture, the people working there will haphazardly create one. Abdicate this essential duty, and you forfeit a leadership tool. Intentionally create a healthy culture, and your team will thrive.

So, what kind of culture do you have? Do you like what you see? Or are you irritated about it? If it's the latter, launch the process of becoming a "cultural architect." The obvious person to assume this role is the key leader of the business, church, or organization.

In addition to being a great leader, Solomon was a cultural architect. Contrast him with King Herod. According to my good friend and experienced Israeli tour guide, Roni Winter, Herod was known as "the king everybody loved to hate." Herod had a knack for architecture and buildings. From the hippodrome and aqueducts of Caesarea Maritima on the coast of the Mediterranean, to the third rebuilding of the temple in Jerusalem and his winter palace at Masada, near the Dead Sea, Herod loved his buildings. In fact, he likely loved them more than the people he led. So much so that he created a culture of fear and suspicion throughout his reign. Nice buildings and a crazy leader are not a good combination.

Culture can also be shaped by those not at the top. Those who have joined our staff through the years learn by what we call "The Inspire Way." We don't expect them to figure it out on their own; we teach it, and they observe it. Once they understand it, they are expected to contribute and protect what is dear to our hearts.

SHAPING YOUR CULTURE

1. DISCOVER WHAT EXISTS

Principle: Identify reality and resolve tensions.

If you are taking over the leadership or management of a previously established culture, the first thing to do in shaping culture is to identify what exists. If you are a young and ambitious start-up, pay attention; you might say, "There's no culture here." Oh, but there is. In the words of Bart Simpson, "Au contraire, mon frere!" (on the contrary, my friend). An unkept culture is like a garden that has sat untended for years. Weeds overgrown and sprouting wild require effort to clean up, root out, and get the garden in decent shape.

The Queen of Sheba has inspired more than thirty restaurant business owners and distribution centers worldwide. Her influence has changed Ethiopian cuisine in more than twenty restaurants in the United States and eight other restaurants in such parts of the world as Israel, Ethiopia, the Netherlands, South Africa, and India.

It's likely you've walked into an office (or even your own home) and felt tension; everyone seemed on edge. If it's an ongoing thing, chances are that tension has made its way into the office culture. Being a pretty high-strung person by nature, I have to coach myself into periodically winding things down a notch because it can create a persona of intensity that isn't good for the team I lead. Sure, they need to know the Inspire Way includes high expectations, but I don't need to add undue pressure that—while some may thrive on it—can fluster others so they aren't able to bring their best selves to work.

If you're trying to build an employment environment where staff can bring an emotional support pet to hide under their desk, or park their personal French press coffee plunger at an open-concept desk, good luck. That may or may not have a positive effect on your environment; it could add distraction. Chances are you're going to do lots of side counseling. If you're giving personal time off or allowing for a "stress day" when you or one of your supervisors is wilting under the pressure of leadership and lacks the emotional intelligence or "grit" that we've heard so much about in the past few years, then you've got your work cut out for you.

You may shy away from facing conflict, the sources of tension, or other elephants in the room, but eventually you must be brutally honest with yourself. You must also allow others to be just as honest with you. If you function in the midst of a toxic environment, call it Chernobyl and fix the toxic problem. The first step to fixing it is to face the music and say, "This has to change." Or, you could soon be saying, "I can't take this anymore," or even worse, "Calgon, take me away!" (If you recognize the phrase, you are likely a child of the 1980s—the real Greatest Generation.)

Once you confront reality, you have taken a step in the right direction. As the late American inventor, General Motors research director, and businessman Charles "Boss" Kettering once said: "A problem well stated is a problem half solved."[8] However, it's not enough to identify the problem. You must have the courage to fight it and change the culture's negative characteristics. While it may take a while to turn the ship around, it's definitely doable.

Nobody wants to come to work in a place where nobody gets along, and everybody wants to do the least amount of work as possible (sounds like an oxymoron). *The least amount of work as possible?* Selecting the right people is crucial—remember to "hire slow, fire fast." In the past two decades, I have had my share of dealing with the damaging effects of disunity. I had to learn how to confront people who weren't performing up to standards, as well as how to push for confrontation to reach a peaceful resolution. You are only as good as your team. But teams are not self-operating, plug-and-play pieces of equipment you can wind up and then walk away from. They need constant coaching, encouragement, and reminders of the values (that should be stated) about who we are, what we do, why we do it—and most importantly—For *whom* we do it.

If your destination for your organization is the absence of conflict (peace) and smooth sailing (a matter of individual per-spective), it must pass through an expensive toll booth named Conflict. We all want peace, but sometimes we want peace at all costs, which leads to a fragile and often unrealistic peace. When we do that, we tolerate things that we shouldn't. We overlook problems and issues and give people a pass because they have seniority, we simply don't like conflict, or we just want people to like us. So, we let it slide.

However, avoiding issues enables those who are directly involved, frustrates others who are part of the organization's inner workings, and confuses those on the periphery. As a necessity, over the years I have learned to handle confrontation with finesse, sometimes even initiating it. Now that I have developed this skill, I will often initiate conflict to achieve a valid, lasting peace. Jesus called us to be peacemakers, not just peacekeepers. Granted, there's still a bit of warrior-like David in me, which means I probably need to develop the more diplomatic nature of Solomon.

Many of us don't like confrontation, but because of that we also don't experience the peace we desire. Art imitates life, and the same could be said for business. In life, we will experience plenty of problems. The plumbing won't work on the third floor, and Mrs. Jones is calling; she's upset. Fix it. The young girl at the counter was rude, and you got two Yelp stars that diminished your overall customer rating. Gently correct her.

Allowing toxicity to continue in a culture means some people either won't deal with the problem when one arises, or they'll just hand it off to someone else who has been specially trained to address it. Leaders who don't want to, or are unsure how to, confront others for fear of fallout sometimes allow things to go unchecked. Then it spreads to other staff members and leaders.

That's what happened to us. First, the wounded bleed and tell their families and closest coworkers. Then it has the potential to breed, spreading in a crazy, pandemic-style fashion. Ultimately, you will face a culture challenge you must tackle head on, and it will begin with the person standing in front of the mirror.

King Solomon's story isn't just for Bible scholars or adults. The wisdom of Solomon is mentioned by Mark Twain in Chapter 14 of The Adventures of Huckleberry Finn.

A few Christmas seasons ago, I took my family to a well-known diner in Honolulu that had been there for at least sixty years—a greasy spoon type of place that locals loved. It brought warmth to your heart, since at its essence the place offered my kind of local comfort food. The waitresses worked extremely hard, too. As a family-owned business, its reputation preceded itself, so the staff were always busy. Interestingly, as a proudly cash-only business, when the COVID-19 crisis hit Hawai'i, it was sadly among the first to close its doors.

As much as I loved their food, I didn't return to this diner after the Christmastime experience I'm about to relate. We sat down at the counter and ordered, but for some reason it took an hour for our food to arrive. In the meantime, I saw people sit down who had ordered fifteen to twenty minutes after we did, but who received their food before we did. After a half hour, I grew a little impatient. Finally, the third time I asked, "Ma'am, do you know if our food is coming out yet?" my voice went up an octave. Within five minutes she dropped our plates in front of us. No bread and butter while we had been waiting or an apology for the lengthy wait. Just plates dropped on the counter and an abrupt turn away from us.

While we were glad to finally get our food, I felt a little guilty. Worried that I had offended the woman in this very busy restaurant, after paying the bill I came back to give her a twenty-dollar bill. Given my experience at The Willows, I understood the pressure she was under. However, she took the folded Andrew Jackson and angrily threw it on the ground, leaving me embarrassed. The guy standing next to me said, "If she don't want it, I'll take it!" and snatched it off the floor, although I recall taking it back. As I walked out, it felt like—to put it mildly—someone had thrown a wet blanket over what should have been an enjoyable evening. Actually, I felt horrible about this exchange and still feel it this day.

All that to pose this question: Should a customer ever be made to feel that way? This restaurant exhibited an inability (to use an overused COVID term) to pivot and change from a cash-only business to a cash-and-credit system. It offered terrible customer service when the pressure was on (and I'm sorry if I didn't know the pressures she faced at work, the personal story behind her life, or the sticky situation she might have faced at home). So, though saddened, I was not surprised when this iconic and historical restaurant closed. Now, it would be unfair of me to paint all the restaurant's personnel with the same broad brushstroke, but it can take just one employee to make a whole organization look bad. I will always remember the famous hamburger steak, served with delicious potato salad and rice smothered in gravy, but my lasting memory is the customer service on my final visit.

2. DETERMINE THE SOURCE OF THE PROBLEM

Principle: Make changes when needed.

If you want to change your culture, start by determining the source of the aggravation. It could be a policy or procedure tripping you up. Or, worse, it could be a person. Or even worse, a whole department. Whatever you discover, you must evaluate the situation and then act. Some struggle to make the changes required once they discover the source (person).

It's like someone who discovers they have diabetes but never returns for another checkup and fails to take their medication or change their diet. This means possibly losing their eyesight, amputation, and even death. The obvious lesson? Make the change.

After removing aggravators, make it clear to others what you don't want your culture to be like and eliminate anything that doesn't line up with your vision and plans. You have to be resolute in your conviction and declare: "That will not be a part of who we are."

Some changes will be difficult. They may involve releasing people not willing to buy into the culture. Rest assured; it will be worth it. After you've done the tough work of eliminating, reinstate vision and the confidence of your team as you protect and guard your culture. With diligence, you can elevate your organization!

3. DEFINE WHAT YOU REALLY WANT

Principle: Good leaders bring clarity to the situation.

Like terrible plumbing, without an intentional approach from leadership, culture settles to the lowest level. If you have difficulty articulating the kind you want, start by articulating what you don't want. That's easy to do. What do you not want your business, church, or organization to be like? After you've come up with a list, write another of what you do want. Close your eyes and complete this sentence: The organization I envision is _____. Simple.

When I became the senior leader, I wish I had started with a more clearly defined culture. I did so with my vision, but not the culture. While I had it in my mind and heart, to document it would have been helpful for everyone. While that wasn't fair, it was the best I knew how to do. So don't just make a note to work on this "someday." Start writing your culture statement now.

Behind every great team is a culture that is articulated, expressed, and taught. Combine these elements, and you will find your team will catch this healthy culture. You will not transfer it by osmosis. People need time and teaching—caught and taught. Once a team is unified in a healthy culture, they will naturally produce victories and get you some Ws as opposed to the Ls. There's no limit to what God can do with a church, business, or organization in that condition.

King Solomon had twenty years to create and curate a culture that was fit for his kingdom. It would be presumptive to assume these values were passed on from his father's court to Solomon's. After all, we have to remember that David was more astute at the art of warfare and strategy and less on hospitality and excellence. Sure, King Saul came before him, the first king this great nation ever had. Prior to that, Israel was made up of twelve loosely affiliated tribes for some three centuries until

David united all of the tribes, much like Genghis Khan would do with the Mongols 1,500 years later, in a much larger expanse of territory. So David might have launched the family business, so to speak, but it would be Solomon who would get it listed on the NASDAQ.

In Saul and David's time, there was probably so much unimaginable bloodshed with a myriad of enemies that it must have made for a nice reprieve when David brought everyone together under one flag. No more individual agendas, and no more fighting for personal preferences. No more this is "my guy" or "my leader" or employee rabble rousing of forces pressing for greater benefits (although I'm all for that; namely, the benefits).

While folks generally loved David, they were over the blood and guts thing. They needed—no, they wanted, indeed craved—stability. They wanted food to eat from the crops they grew. They wanted the "fat of the land" in the land of "milk and honey." Namely, they wanted livestock (which would bring milk and meat) and honey (trees that blossomed and produced fruit, the pollination of flowers and trees, and the birds and the bees). I think you get my point.

This is why the latter years of David's reign brought a breath of fresh air to Israel. When he ended his corporate takeover of other nations—total dominance of the enemies surrounding Israel—he absorbed their assets and built the country's wealth and financial reserves. But before David died, he raised up an Elon Musk-sort of son and set him up to take the family business and make it into a regional juggernaut.

Solomon, the son-of-a-boss/king, would take the family fortunes and succeed. He dealt with his father's old enemies and any future rivals to his throne. With ruthless sophistication, the new king had his men carry out his orders. Solomon had a next-level gene in him that his brothers didn't have. It would not just differentiate him or distance him. It would distinguish Solomon, so he could begin to build, create, and curate what the Queen of Sheba would experience.

EXCELLENCE IN THE CULTURE

When it comes to spreading a contagious culture, sometimes you must act quickly, knowing in the long run it will be worth the effort.

04

J ust before I started working on this book, I turned to Lisa and told her we needed to create a new staff member orientation program that included a field trip to Inspire's original home. "We'll break up our values and spread them across four one-hour teachings," I said with a finger in the air and a smile on my face. "It will end with putting them all in a van and driving them to the spot where our church first met."

Considering the thousands who now identify with our church, you may shrug, "So what?" That is, until you appreciate the story of our beginnings: forty people with little more to our names than big dreams, living on the razor's edge between faith and fear, and a few thousand dollars in the bank. Plus, two laptops and two Nextel phones, which I dubbed our "Next to Hell" phones because the walkie-talkie feature regularly interfered with phone calls. This is the story I plan to share with new hires as I drive them to our very first "office"—a loft over the second floor of a good friend's cabinet business, *tucked away in an industrial area just outside of Honolulu. I want to share with newcomers that great places, spaces, and architecture, as well as stretching and believing for more, don't always happen. No matter what the outcome, though, there is always a humble beginning.*

THE ELEMENTS

There's another reason I got so charged up about this new idea: Culture isn't just about what you want and what you don't want. Actually, that's the easy part. Having a list of cultural values on your office wall won't change your culture. That's too easy and will almost always fail. The hard part about culture is that it has to be taught and caught. Even then, your work is never done. It always requires culture to be (or to have been) . . .

1) Transmitted: constantly teaching in formal and semi-formal environments.

2) Translated: it has a sound and language all its own. Timely: communication excellence in . . . communicating. Transferable: passed down at every level with "culture carriers" so that it is repeatable and duplicatable. Thorough: includes debriefing, a time to make corrections. Debriefing requires things to be thought through well so as to disseminate the details, dissect the issues, make corrections off the findings to produce a better product, and improve the system.

CULTURE MUST BE TRANSMITTED

Culture must be transmitted. In other words, it must be taught and transferred to the hearers. The information cascades from the top to the bottom as it is both *delivered* and *received*. This is a key reason for wanting our new staff members to catch a vision of where we started and how far we have come and to develop an appreciation for what our culture has helped build.

This transmittal of vision is similar to a sales transaction: A seller must ship a product, so the recipient or purchaser can receive it (unless it has been lost in transit, delayed, or stolen).

Culture cannot be taught on the fly. It must have a formal and an informal setting. In the latter it can be caught, but first it must be taught. This teaching cannot be administered by a junior staff member or delegated to another executive or administrator. The person who cares the most about the culture is the one who should be doing the teaching. Namely, the person at the top (CEO, owner, or senior pastor) whenever possible. As I mentioned in Chapter Three, in the past I was guilty of not teaching this myself and delegating the job to someone else. Now, while I'm sure that person did a better-than-average job, this is a case of "If you want it done right (or in a particular way), you have to do it yourself."

I've already mentioned *Excellence Wins* by Horst Schulze, the former CEO of the Ritz-Carlton Hotels. One reason I admired this book is his great candor and the insight he offers about the importance of the senior leader conducting orientation sessions for new hires. Then Schulze goes a level deeper by discussing the importance of perpetuating the teaching by living out those values. Those are the practices that helped make the Ritz-Carlton brand of hotels what it is to this day—a worldwide network of approximately 100 hotels, many ranked in the upper echelons of their country's "Best Hotel" surveys.

Before I read Schulze's captivating book and changed the way I handle orientations, we were already starting our days the right way. From 9:00 to 9:15 every morning (Tuesday through Friday) we gathered the staff, so someone could share about one of our core values and offer a story or Scripture passage, plus an encouragement based on that value. Then we would pray, and everyone got to work.

When a staff member hears those things repeatedly—a minimum of four times per week—and rotates through them and the entire set of values at least ten times a year, they tend to sink in and grow roots. Any other challenges we encounter often don't stem from a violation of our values, but reflect personal struggles. And just like any church member, staff members (including me) need pastoring, too. So these sessions help eliminate different agendas and curb the various personal problems that can hurt the organization as a whole. We are constantly trying to reinforce our core values, in formal and informal settings. The second can be done informally, in a sidebar conversation, while doing a task, or using a mistake as a teachable moment. Always look for opportunities to reinforce your stated values.

CULTURE MUST BE TRANSLATED

Because culture has a language of its own, new staff coming into the organization must be brought up to speed on your organization's "lingo." Language shapes culture and reinforces it as well. The wrong language will give you something you never intended to create. It can also undermine and deteriorate what you have built. Casual language around products and services can create an aura of slackness when you're trying to build something far more professional.

Years ago, as a younger staff member at another church, I had a testy conversation—rather than a calm interaction—with someone from a cell phone company. I had disputed some charges on my bill and was growing increasingly frustrated with my apparent lack of progress. To put it mildly, I became less than graceful as we talked. Just then, one of the executive pastors, who would be comparable to a CFO in business, overheard me as he walked by my office. When I finished, he called me into his office and asked me to close the door behind me. Years later, I don't recall the exact words he used, but he definitely got his message across: My conduct on the phone had been less than honorable. It would especially reflect poorly on the church as a whole if the rep at the cell phone company learned the identity of my employer. The way I conducted business was hurting the brand. I totally got it and expressed remorse. Message received.

Ironically, after I became the senior leader at our church, I encountered the same issue with another staff member. Now in those days, we had office cubicles, the kind designed so you can hear every conversation going on around you. Although I didn't know who the staff member was talking to, they were doing the same thing I had done a decade earlier. Being on the other end of the situation, with the shoe on the other foot, I was aghast at the staff member's behavior. When the conversation ended, I did the same thing that the CFO did for me. I brought the person into my office, and we reviewed what had been transferred to me in my younger days, making this a teachable moment. She tried to excuse it: "Oh, but I know her; I've been working with her for months on this issue," to which I replied, "I understand, but in this case it doesn't matter. You will be overheard by other employees and worse yet, other volunteers in the office within earshot who heard every part of your conversation." She was remorseful, and as far as I know, it never happened again.

When it comes to living out our values, the language we use is critical. Treating people with honor and respect is important. Regardless of the circumstances or the context, we've got to be aware that the language we use, as well as our tone and our tenor, say much about our level of excellence—or lack of it. So, what we say and how we say it carries considerable weight. Some might argue the church is not a business, so we have a level of spiritual authority that allows us to flex our spiritual muscles whenever necessary. Ordinarily, I might tend to agree with that sentiment. But that is done in very few cases. In other words, seldom exercised. Imagine if you have a staff of fifty people who have learned such behavior, and think they can pull that card out every once in a while. Can you see the compounding effects that will have on the organization? Exactly.

Let's face it. We are going to face times throughout the week when we will not be at our best. Our A-game got left at home. But we still must be able to put our feelings aside and serve people well. That's why language and teaching people the right way to represent the heart of your organization and giving them the right phrases and words to say is so important. That way, it's as though you speak with one voice in the midst of great diversity. We all might have differences of opinions, but at the end of the day, we must speak with a curated language that honors God, loves people, and is done in an excellent manner.

Classical composer George Frideric Handel wrote an oratorio (a large musical composition for orchestra, choir, and singers) on the biblical stories of Solomon, including an act on the Queen of Sheba.

This is where in recent years, we have become more like Solomon. As I might have said before, I'm more of a warrior, a sort of rough-and-tumble, plain-speaking, tell-it-like-it-is kind of guy. But that doesn't work everywhere. The Bible tells us to season our conversation with words of wisdom and grace, so they are like apples of gold set on a silver platter (as Proverbs puts it). I would rather receive an apple of gold on a silver platter than a fresh apple (wisdom) served up on the lid of a trash can. How about you? In other words, in order for our words to have the effectiveness we require, we need to be tactful. I often remind myself and coach my staff on using *finesse* in our conversations. This avoids offending someone and can defuse an unsatisfied customer.

CULTURE COMMUNICATION MUST BE TIMELY

I think one of the most frustrating things in trying to create a culture of excellence boils down to achieving successful communication. We are either communicating well—or we are not. This is one of the areas where it is difficult to find middle ground. As famed Irish playwright George Bernard Shaw once put it: "The single biggest problem in communication is the illusion that it has taken place."[9]

Part of the Inspire Way has to do with our internal communications; the other half of the equation is external. The latter is the easy part. When it comes to social media posts, database email responses, and other communications with the public, I think proper grammar and succinctness are important. The creative marketing team must curate the essentials to these posts. Emails should be answered within twenty-four hours in a specific way with a greeting and a salutation at the end, all done with professionalism. The organization must sound like it speaks with one voice versus several voices of the handful of staff members tasked that day with writing emails. That doesn't look or sound professional at all. There has to be consistency. As with other standards, in the past, we have been guilty of *inconsistency*.

External communications include the timeliness of replying to voicemails left on the phone, the way that we answer the phone, and the specific verbiage we use. For example, this is the way I was taught to answer the phone at my first church: "Thank you for calling Hope Chapel; this is Mike speaking. How may I help you?" In the early days of Inspire, I would call the church office just to see how team members would answer the phone. (I think I should do that all over again, just to test the system.)

LEVELS OF COMMUNICATION:

Face-to-Face—When it comes to the levels of communication, the highest form is face-to-face. In most cases when it comes to customer service this is a given and a standard operating procedure. But outside of the hospitality industry, this is not always the case. Whenever possible, this is what we want to achieve.

Teleconference—Communication cascades downward. So, the next form is through a teleconference. Since the pandemic, Zoom sessions and quick FaceTime catch-ups have achieved great progress. Now most of my doctor's appointments are done via telemedicine. Another important level in communication is picking up the phone and making a call. Even if you don't get through, you can leave a message.

Email—The next level of communication is what we seem to spend most of our time on, and that's crafting emails and replying to staff members and customers alike.

Text messages—And then the lowest form of communication is a text message. The challenge is that this is the easiest and most efficient method. Group texting gets things done more quickly as we move at the speed of our broadbands. But it is still the lowest form when it comes to individual communication. These different levels are important to remember because they each have their own protocol. For example, when it comes to text messages, it is important to reply as soon as possible. Nothing is worse than to feel like your text has been ignored. There is no room for "okay" or "yeah" or replying like a teenager. We answer one another with respectful greetings like, "Got it" or "Sure thing" or "No problem." It's the small things that mean a lot.

In cases when we have attempted to get in touch with someone (vendor, customer, or client), there have been times when I've asked staff members how many times and in what different ways did they attempt to make contact. However, internal communications are just as critical. So, we have this mantra or saying: "Circle back, follow through, and close the loop" (which we recognize by the acronym, CBFTCTL). To define that further:

Circle back—Simply put, revisiting a subject or finding an answer to a question and following up with someone: "Hi, Steve, I just wanted to *circle back* on your request . . ."

Follow through—You can have a high-powered offense and a great football team, but if you seem to get stuck in the red zone (between the twenty-yard line and the goal line) and rarely get the ball into the end zone, you're not going to win many games. In communications, this is the equivalent of someone dropping the ball and nobody being there to pick it up. That is definitely cause for frustration. In the fast-paced world in which we live, we often forget a particular task. As time goes by, it may seem everyone's forgotten, or some people are satisfied because the boss hasn't brought it up in a while. But when he does, it's not going to be good when he remembers: "Hi, Steve, I wanted to circle back to see if you had *followed through* on Mrs. Jones's request . . . ."

Close the loop—This is when communication has been successfully accomplished or an issue has been put to rest. This is done so that everybody is on the same page, and we are able to move on with other important items on the agenda: "Hi, John, this is Steve. I just wanted to *circle back* with you to let you know that I had *followed through* on Mrs. Jones's request, and she is happy and well taken care of. Thank you for your patience and cooperation. I just wanted to *close the loop* on her request. Have a great day!"

Almost every time something has not been executed well the communication bottleneck has occurred in one or more of these three key areas. And when that happens, you will often find me texting the following: "#CBFTCTL?" I might add to the text: "Live it, learn it, love it."

CULTURE HAS TRANSFERABLE QUALITIES

Culture moves quicker when it is transferred through those within the organization who have bought into the cultural vision. One of the ways a culture can be curated, cultivated, and transferred is through people who are carriers—someone who has what you want everybody to have. Relax, I'm not talking about a deadly virus! What I mean is people who carry the culture of your organization. In our context, they embrace the Inspire Way. They are able to reflect, embody, and articulate the intangibles of our culture in such a way that, at the least, it makes people take notice of it, and at best, capture it.

One of the worst things that can happen is when someone who should be a culture carrier is actually spreading something different—especially the wrong message. For volunteer-driven organizations like a church, this is quite tricky. The reason I say this is because, for a volunteer, there is no financial incentive, no paycheck linked to buying into the core values. They have to be inspired without any noticeable reward, other than the betterment of their personal and professional lives.

King David did not pass his kingdom down
to his firstborn as was customary during
that time. Instead, he passed the throne
down to his tenth son, Solomon.[10]

However, I can point to many people in the marketplace who have soaked up the cultural values of our church and applied them to their own context. It goes without saying that all of our cultural values come from biblical principles. But those who have benefited from them have taken these values and principles and after sitting in weekend services, listening to our podcasts and other online content, and sitting under our training for months (sometimes years), have been able to creatively adapt these teachings to their own environments. It has benefited them professionally, personally, financially, and—most of all—spiritually. Carriers don't just appear; they are coached. Yet this investment of time pays incredible dividends.

One of the most adept groups at inculcating the idea of culture is the national rugby union team from New Zealand known as the All Blacks. The team represents the nation in international competition. Because it's considered the country's national sport, and because they're the all-time winningest sports team, the All Blacks are heroes in their homeland. Since their debut in the late nineteenth century and their entry into international competition, they have become known for their unparalleled success. After entering international competition, from 1903 through 2019, they posted a winning record of just over seventy-seven percent of their international rugby tests. They were the first team to win five 500 test matches and have three World Cups to their name.

The All Blacks have several advantages, the most obvious being their athletic talent. Their captains are legendary, achieving household name status outside New Zealand in such countries as Australia, Great Britain, and South Africa.

Secondly, they follow the traditional Maori protocol called the *haka*. If you've never seen it before, go to this YouTube link and watch it (https://www.youtube.com/watch?v=PptTeyYShdw). The *haka* is so inspiring on one hand and intimidating on the other. Often, by the time the *haka* reaches its crescendo, the test is almost decided. Each opposing team handles it differently; some will ignore it and look above the team, while others will stand boldly, shoulder-to-shoulder with their teammates, and defiantly withstand it. Personally, I am surprised at the teams that allow them to chant their *haka* when the All Blacks are the visitors. And yet, the most important characteristic of this team is not the *haka*, but the culture that they have built over the years.

In *Legacy*, his bestselling book about the team, author James Kerr shares fifteen key cultural values that have made the All Blacks so successful over a long period of time. Now you might be wondering, *What does this have to do with customer service?* Nothing. But it has everything to do with a culture that is carefully curated over a long period of time, bringing about lasting success and sustainability. That is a truth worth pondering by every organization and its leaders. While I won't review all fifteen of these cultural values—or what Kerr calls fifteen "elegant mantras"—it's quite likely that adopting these values will help you as well.

We live in an athletic world featuring highly paid, free-agent athletes who understandably will either play for the highest bidder or form a kind of super-PAC to play for a team for up to three (possibly as many as five) years in their quest for a championship ring. The contrarian approach of the All Blacks' success is this: "No one is bigger than the team, and individual brilliance doesn't automatically lead to outstanding results. One selfish mindset will infect a collective culture," Kerr writes.[11]

Elsewhere, he observes that fundamental human drive comes from within—from intrinsic rather than extrinsic motivations:

> *"Leaders who harness the power of purpose have the ability to galvanize a group, aligning its behaviours to the strategic pillars of the enterprise. Using vivid storytelling techniques, including themes, symbols, imagery, rituals, mantras and metaphor, and bringing them to life with imagination and flair, leaders create a sense of inclusion, connectedness and unity—a truly collective, collaborative mindset. It begins by asking 'Why? Why are we doing this? Why am I sacrificing myself for this project? What is the higher purpose?' The answers to these questions have the ability to transform the fortunes of a group or enterprise—activating individuals, providing a cultural glue, guiding behaviours and creating an overall sense of purpose and personal connection. It is the beginning of the being of team."*[12]

Not just a team, I might add. On the All Blacks rugby squad, everyone is expected to be a carrier of the culture. In fact, to their organization, you are part of the team "24-7." This exemplifies

Jim Collins's *Good to Great* spirit of "who before what" and "we before me."

CULTURE MUST BE THOROUGH

This section can also be called "debriefing." A debrief requires a follow-up session to carefully think through things in a thorough fashion. This is a time for the entire team to disseminate details, dissect issues, discuss and break down conversations, and analyze how they could have been done better; all of this attention to detail helps build a culture of excellence. We take a thorough approach to much of what we do.

I learned about the necessity of debriefing from another pastor in Hawai'i. His church's culture included this practice. They had a culture of excellence, although in their early days they got a bad rap because of it, especially when critics labeled it "perfectionism." That wasn't a fair assessment, even though this prominent church pushed the envelope when it came to excellence. They were just outstanding and had raised the bar of how a church can present its services. It was polished and professional, and at the same time so heartfelt, that it was one of the original inspirations for Inspire to emulate and copy, to some extent.

Of course, in our early years—with the talent we had and my level of preaching and teaching not where it is today—we couldn't compete with their flair. At one time, they were the largest church in the state, and to this day they still have incredible influence. One of their elements of genius was instilling this culture of debrief. It's all about improving the system, structures, and services you provide.

After every midweek service or weekend of services, they would debrief. Everybody who played a key role in the production was part of these discussions. During these sessions, they talked about what went well, what didn't, and how they could improve. Their goal was simple: to become better and better. I don't think people in church in Hawai'i back in those days were used to that kind of painstaking effort. It was the old fight of quality versus quantity ("Oh, we have quality while they focus on quantity.") and "good enough" was worn like a badge of honor in those days. People weren't used to a level of excellence in debrief that they brought to the state. It definitely made them better, and we intentionally transferred that value onto us as well.

What would it look like if you debriefed more often with staff members? Why wait until a year-end review to let someone know how they're doing? Why not let them know as soon as possible, so they can implement the changes? This also goes with something that I value personally: coaching people in real time. Sometimes I'm pressed for time and can't afford to wait for a debriefing session to tell someone how they did or how we can improve. A basketball coach doesn't just wait until halftime to make necessary adjustments. He's making them on the fly as he shouts out instructions and encouragement to his team from the sidelines in real time. When it comes to spreading a contagious culture, sometimes you must act quickly, knowing in the long run it will be worth the effort.

part two

SEE LIKE THE QUEEN OF SHEBA: CREATIVE
ADAPTATION & CULTURAL CONTEXTUALIZATION

05: See The Hard Truths

06: See The Potential

SEE THE HARD TRUTHS

What people say about your business is critical to your business.

05

What people say about your business is important to your business. That's why we must be really good listeners. If we opt to put our heads in the sand and ignore what people are saying—whether good or bad—then we will miss teachable moments and golden opportunities to become better at what we do.

For any organization (nonprofit, business, church), I can see where a focused determination or resiliency to remain "true to who we are and what we are called to be" holds the potential to backfire. The cold hard facts today are that organizations can fail to appreciate that people are coming into their environment with certain standards for customer service etched in their minds. Careless (or no) greetings, shoddy facility appearance, and a general lackadaisical attitude toward visitors leave the impression that the hosts could not care less whether newcomers are there or not. Church leaders and CEOs need an awareness of such an outlook and to become savvier in this area.

Please don't misunderstand me: As the pastor of a church, I'm not saying we should cater to those who embrace a "consumer Christianity." Nor am I negating the importance of people who feel called to a particular church or who identify with a particular pastor and are willing to *overlook any obvious flaws along their journey. After all, if anyone wants to look hard enough, they can find all kinds of faults with any church, all day long, and easily pick it apart. While I don't advocate kowtowing to such armchair critics, we still must pay attention to what people are saying.*

SOUR SERVICE

This topic is fresh on my mind since it took place in early 2021 on a vacation to Southern California. During our search for a place where we could order dinner, some friends had recommended a great Japanese restaurant just a mile up the coast from where we were staying. They told us it served the best sushi in Orange County. Besides this personal recommendation, you have to appreciate that I love Japanese food. If I were ever given a "last meal" before I checked out permanently, you can bet I would choose this form of cuisine.

After finding the phone number and address, I opted to drive over myself instead of summoning Uber Eats or Grubhub. Since we were in the early days of the vaccine rollout, in my eyes the fewer people who handled our food the better. When I got to the restaurant, the ambiance was great. The face-to-face conversation and customer service couldn't have been better. Although the bill was higher than I expected, I took the server's word for it when she told me everything I had ordered was in the package. I even added a generous twenty percent tip (really undeserved because the waitstaff didn't do much, compared to pre-COVID days) before hopping into my rental car and driving back to the hotel.

When I opened the package, I discovered several mistakes, starting with the fact they got part of my order wrong. Nor were there any chopsticks, which are essential to enjoying the Asian food experience (just ask my Chinese-born wife). In fact, there weren't any kind of utensils. It's a good thing we had forks of our own. Imagine if we had decided to go to the beach to enjoy our dinner while lounging on the sand and watching the sunset. Not good when you've just ordered hot soup with noodles. Plus, amongst the three different types of sauces they gave us, the most important one was missing: the soy sauce. The wasabi was there, but in my estimation—despite the food critics who insist the two should never be mixed—wasabi is no good without the soy sauce. Add them up: 1) partially wrong order, 2) no chopsticks, and 3) no soy sauce. In my book, the triple play of cardinal sins for Japanese food takeout had been committed.

So, I called the restaurant back; the same girl who took my order answered the phone. In a kind and understanding voice, I explained to her that I just wanted to let her to know about the mistake in my order, including the missing utensils, which could help them "for future reference." Rather than thanking me, she replied in a rather curt tone of voice, "You're welcome to drive back and pick up some chopsticks."

LOL! I thought to myself. *That's not going to happen because by this time I'm already eating my once was hot but now is lukewarm dinner. Driving over there for chopsticks would mean my dinner would definitely be too cold to enjoy.*

Of course, the correct response from that female would have been a profuse apology and an attempt to correct the problem and make things right with a paying customer. Instead, after telling me in a monotone voice I could come back to get some chopsticks, she hung up. That's right, she . . . Straight. Up. Hung. Up. On. Me! Now, what followed is not my normal course of business, but on a twelve-day vacation that took us through two states I had faced too much of this. Namely, subpar customer service and what I felt was an "entitlement" attitude projected by too many waitstaff who had taken our orders—as well as management. So, I did what I almost never do: expressed my frustration on Yelp about this particular restaurant because *what people say about your business is important to your business.*

CORRECTIVE ACTION

Bear with me; I don't want to lose you by belaboring too many details of what happened and come off as some kind of prima donna. It's important to understand the context of this scenario, especially because of what happened next. Now, this great Japanese restaurant had been getting great reviews on Yelp, which were at odds with what had just happened to us. When I proceeded through the app and left my review, I didn't go off on them or offer harsh, biting criticisms. I simply spelled out the facts of our order and the resulting blasé reaction from the waitstaff when I called.

Long after this happened, what still impresses me more than anything was that within an hour of my post the general manager reached back to me on Yelp. He apologized and wanted additional details about what had gone wrong, what time I had been there, and my interaction with his team. After several more apologies and even asking for my number so he could send me a certificate for my next meal at one of their two establishments, he had won me back as a customer.

Even though King David anointed King Solomon to take the throne, the transfer of power was anything but smooth. Solomon's older brother, Adonijah, initially tried to usurp the throne but conceded after David officially made Solomon king.

I graciously declined his gesture of a gift card, because I wasn't Yelping in hopes of getting a reward. I wanted to help this general manager use our interaction and conversation as a teachable moment for his team. I surely hope nobody got fired because that wasn't my intent. I simply wanted to help him capitalize on an opportunity to help his businesses excel. Let's face it, you can have the best sushi chefs, great food, and expensive COVID upgrades to make people feel safe, but if your customer service is lacking or even sucks (Can I say that?), then you may not stay in business for very long. Going on Yelp should help the management hear what people are saying—good or bad.

Yet what happens most of the time? According to one survey, seventy-nine percent of customers who share complaints online see them ignored, and eighty-four percent report their expectations *had not* been exceeded in their last interaction with customer service. In 2019, nearly half of American consumers switched companies because of poor customer service; overall, eighty-two percent of customers have ceased doing business with a company for this reason. And, ninety-one percent of customers who had a bad customer experience won't willingly do business with that company again. This is the bottom line: Businesses can increase revenue between 4-8 percent above their market when they prioritize better customer service.[13]

Because the manager of this Japanese restaurant paid attention to my complaint and exceeded my expectations in the way he resolved the issue, after talking with him I deleted my post on Yelp. Since he had taken care of everything in an expeditious manner, there was no need to leave my complaint up there. This manager should be commended. He understands the truth of this chapter: What people say *about your business* is critical *to your business*. One company that specializes in providing customer service software found that customers are willing to spend thirty-one percent more on a business with excellent online reviews, while ninety-four percent say an online review convinced them to avoid a business. Four of five consumers have changed their minds about a recommended purchase after reading negative online reviews.

Previously, I wrote that what people are saying about your business or nonprofit is your *brand*. You can pay thousands in trying to curate your brand while not paying attention to the fact that what people say about you actually *is* your brand. I know; it seems a bit unfair. And it's out there, whether you like it or not. People are talking and have opinions (like I do) and platforms and opportunities to express them in positive and negative ways. Thanks to social media, smartphones, and other high-tech tools, more ways than ever exist. Given that fact, it is our responsibility to *listen*.

SENSORY OVERLOAD

When the Queen of Sheba settled into her six-star (a cut above five-star) accommodations, she was on sensory overload. The warm, formal greeting she received at the entrance to the palace made her heart warm with pride over the way she and her entourage had been honored. The queen didn't overlook how her people had been treated with more respect than customarily offered, presented gifts, and offered cool drinks—plus, escorted to their guest quarters.

As she lounged in the tub of her luxurious guest suite and peered out the window that overlooked the palace Solomon had built and the nearby temple, she contemplated how their long journey had been worth every step and every bump on her camel's back. In one sense, she did not want to leave; she could stay there forever. But in another, she knew there were already things back home she wanted to implement. Her kingdom and her vast wealth were already established. It wasn't as if she needed more. Still, she knew *there was more*.

As her attendant sat quietly behind her, waiting on her every wish or command—or even acting as a sounding board and advisor—she began to list several things she wanted to change as soon as she returned home. As the water temperature cooled, her hosts added more hot water, pushing and swirling the rose petals at the top of the surface. As gentle breezes from the Mediterranean Sea flowed into her suite, even the sound of the slowly dripping water pipe fascinated her.

Even though she came from a royal family, the Queen of Sheba was nervous about meeting the legendary king of Israel. All that she had heard about him had spoken volumes to her, even before she had a chance to meet him. Of course, she had questions, but she did not come just to interrogate Solomon or to pose some wily test to see if his answer lived up to his reputation. This was not about experience; she was not meeting the Jeff Bezos or Elon Musk of her day. This was all about learning more of Solomon's wisdom—straight-up wisdom from God to a man who in the future would write a good portion of the Old Testament, from Proverbs to the Song of Solomon to Ecclesiastes.

When she shook herself out of her daydream, she only had a few hours before entering the banquet hall for dinner. The next day had already been planned out for her, including meetings with King Solomon and a tour of the grand city of Jerusalem. She was about to see all that she had heard and learn in detail why she had traveled so far.

GOOD ENOUGH VERSUS EXCELLENCE

One of the biggest challenges of offering superior customer service is combating the mindset—it's an ingrained philosophy of life millions have learned—that we should only strive for "good enough." We can look at floors that don't shine and harbor stray flecks of dirt and shrug that it's good enough. We can look at the dingy toilets in our restaurant and see water spots on the mirror or smell air tinged with a musty odor and walk away thinking, *It's good enough*. We can apply that to every area of our lives, but if we're going to shoot for good enough as the bar of achievement, then we are destined to fail. I don't want good enough results, good enough attitudes, or even average results and attitudes. The enemies to excellence are *good enough* and *average*. Here are five leading reasons why:

1) FIRST IMPRESSIONS MAKE A LASTING IMPRESSION

As I said previously, you only get one chance to make a first impression. Now, your first impression is one thing, but you have to go further in order to win. You must become the other person's favorite until the order is complete, the order has been filled, the product is taken home, and the customer is satisfied. You don't want to just make a good first impression. You want to leave a positive lasting impression.

So, if we are listening to our customers or congregants, we will realize a great opportunity to capitalize on their feedback. If the general manager of that Japanese restaurant had not reached out to me, then it would have validated for me that nobody cared. I would have been among the seventy-nine percent who see their online comments ignored and decided they were not an organization that valued their customers. Absent that manager's contact, did you see how quickly I could have reached those conclusions? That's human nature, almost instantly making negative assumptions. Granted, I may not know the entire context of how their business is run, but based on my first impression, they failed. However, because of the additional feedback and the manager taking ownership of the situation, apologizing, and even offering an extra meal, he did an incredible job of making something right out of something that had gone wrong.

It is widely speculated that King Solomon became King of Israel between the ages of fifteen and twenty.

That's why it's so important for us to pay attention to the feedback and not be overly sensitive about it. Especially in the church world, we have thousands of people who can be difficult to please because much of their experience is subjective and intangible. We don't have a product or a meal to sell. I think that's why we take it more personally when we receive negative feedback. But we can't do that. As my friend Chris Hodges—founding pastor of one of the nation's most influential churches—says, "We don't have to be the best, but we have to be their favorite." So, negative feedback always has a silver lining. We don't have to receive everything, but we can receive something from what is being said if we are willing to listen.

Given the right budget and tools, anyone can "wow!" someone in the beginning, but it's a waste of time and resources if we do not consistently deliver at a level of excellence at every turn of the corner. Excellence cannot be turned on and off like a light switch; it should always be in the on position. You must strive to build a culture with excellence in it so people care about what they do and whom they do it for. They should realize if the organization gets better, they get better. If the organization makes more profits, then they can share in the profits. If the organization gets more esteem and praise, then they will feel proud about being a part of something that is making a lasting impression. Not a *once was*, or a *has been*, or even a *cautionary tale*, but something special that spans the test of time and is COVID-proof.

Let's endeavor to build churches, businesses, and organizations that show off the Creator's creative genius and inspiration in what we do because of our excellence, and let's continue to go to the next level in every area. Let's build something that can handle and endure shifting economies and geopolitical adjustments. Something that is not just weatherproof, but even pandemic proof. It has to leave a lasting impression, and it starts with our teams and our people.

A relevant side note: Did you know the word *inspire* is actually a biblical term? The New Testament was written in the Greek language, the common language of that time period and used throughout the Roman world. The Greek interpretation for inspire is *theopneustos*. It is literally translated as *God-breathed* or *breath of God*. So, whenever you are inspired, it is God-breathed!

2) FAILURE TO MEET EXPECTATIONS
OR EXCEED THEM

The Queen of Sheba would soon find out that Solomon's wisdom and everything he had built would blow away her expectations. Everybody has expectations—certain standards of excellence that is either spoken or unspoken. We walk into a restaurant, a church, or a business establishment, and we all have expectations. We may not have articulated them, but it is undeniable that they exist.

The question is whether we deliver on people's expectations based on our assumptions, or do we take those assumptions and go above and beyond people's expectations? Are we getting a "wow!" or a "meh"? I wonder what emojis the queen would have used if she had them in her day? Would it have been the one with the mind blown, the bunny waving his arms and jumping in the air, or the hearts in the eyes? In fact, it sounds like there were not enough emojis or words to express her feelings; 1 Kings 10:5 talks about taking her breath away. She was at a loss for words. Today she would summarize her reaction as #NoWords. She was indeed speechless. Who does that? Who has the ability to amaze a queen? Solomon.

Part of exceeding expectations is the anticipation factor. Are we listening and attentive, even eavesdropping on our customers' desires and wishes? Today more than ever, it's not one-size-fits-all. It's the flexibility to allow someone to order something that isn't on the menu or simply accommodating a special adjustment in the normal combo lunch special. Anticipation and flexibility are key. They were important in the past, but in twenty-first century reality, they are imperative.

3) RESPONSIVENESS AND OWNERSHIP

I was thankful for the level of response of the general manager at that Japanese restaurant. Now, having been trained at places like the Honolulu Airport and The Willows, it's what I expected. But I'm still thankful he paid attention to the Yelp account. He was responsive and attentive to my needs. As I said earlier, he took a wrong, fixed it, and made it right. That's what we should do: Alleviate the problem and speak into the process so that we can prevent situations like these from happening in the future.

The general manager took ownership. He acted like the owner would have if the owner were in the manager's shoes at that very moment. That's why he's the GM, and that's what he does. Such a sense of ownership has to cascade down to every employee so they will own whatever the problem is, address it, respond appropriately, and alleviate the problem or frustration. To build a culture of excellence, we can't allow people to embrace a mentality of, "That's not my job," or "Let me find someone in that department to help you." We must empower people to act in real time to fix the problem in a manner that will not just meet but exceed their expectations. The general manager exceeded my expectations when he offered me a gift certificate to make things right. (Now I'm wishing I had taken him up on it!)

4) FEEDBACK AND FOLLOW-UP

When it comes to making things right, I think most people stop after taking the first three steps. They will look at making lasting impressions, try to exceed expectations, and strive to be responsive. However, the business that follows up with customer surveys to get additional feedback is the business that will do well—if they use that information to their advantage. Customers don't want to be tested with too many emails or required to respond too often. Still, gestures of interest are always noted. Follow up with people to see how their experience went and gather feedback and you will succeed in making a lasting impression.

5) REPUTATION AND REFERRALS

I started off this chapter talking about your brand and how your brand is what people say about you. So if you're developing a good reputation (AKA brand), then you are going to get referrals. Keep in mind, a couple of friends recommended that restaurant to us, and it initially failed to deliver. But the restaurant did make it right. Will I be referring others to this restaurant again and visiting it myself in the future? Of course I will, because in resolving my complaint, the manager exceeded my expectations. I withdrew my complaint because I wanted to protect the reputation of his business. After all, we all live off referrals.

What are people saying about your business or your church? What are they saying about your customer service and your culture? The only way you will know the truth is if you welcome the feedback. Sometimes the truth hurts, but most of the time the truth helps—if you let it.

SEE THE POTENTIAL

The way you carry yourself and the hard work and determination in which you operate speaks volumes to people.

06

At the time, lacking the benefit of maturity and experience, I didn't appreciate what a risky move Dad made when he left behind nearly two decades in law enforcement. He moved to the hospitality industry to become the security director of the Hawaiian Holiday Macadamia Nut Company, one of many macadamia nut producers on the islands. The industry's origins go back to the late 1800s, when a sugar plantation investor imported nut trees to help protect his sugar cane crops from high winds. Later, the state's agricultural experiment station recommended them as a supplemental industry for coffee growers, leading to the formation of the first macadamia nut company in 1922.

At the time, the Hawaiian Holiday Macadamia Nut Company was riding the wave of popularity that surged in the 1950s after America's love affair with these tasty morsels blossomed. Dad's bosses—owners Paul and Anita De Domenico—placed great trust in him and gave him considerable leeway in his responsibilities. My father has some incredible stories of the people whom he hosted before taking on other responsibilities with the company. The De Domenicos were well known throughout the state, with Anita achieving minor celebrity status in 1977 when she compiled a company cookbook, titled My Macadamia Nut Recipes.

The wealthy couple threw some incredible parties, with Dad hosting and arranging security and travel for people like the governor of Hawai'i. Plus, famous *actors and actresses of the 1970s and '80s, such as Florence Henderson* (The Brady Bunch), *Tim Conway* (The Carol Burnett Show), *Jim Nabors* (Gomer Pyle), *and Carol Burnett herself, to name just a few. One time he hosted the crown prince of Morocco, who had two Moroccan rugs shipped to my dad personally to express his appreciation for the way my father had served him. Plus, he gave him a free helicopter tour of the island (and helicopter tours here can run several hundred dollars an hour). Dad helped to epitomize and perpetuate Hawaiian hospitality and the vision that the owners had established. Although the Hawaiian Holiday company no longer exists, it left a lasting impression on myself and on the many who encountered the De Domenicos and their staff.*

PRINCIPLE 1: WHAT PEOPLE SAY MATTERS

Today one can read about the kind of hospitality and accommodations visitors to Hawai'i enjoy on sites like TripAdvisor or Yelp, all at the flick of a finger. But what attracted the Queen of Sheba's interest in traveling north so far came solely from what she had heard. We will do well to remember the ancient world had no internet, smartphones, or other high-tech tools to check out some place virtually prior to leaving on a trip. It had no brochures, no Kodak moments, and no Facebook or Instagram selfies to provide an idea of what that experience would be like. Everything traveled via word of mouth, from traveler to traveler and messenger to messenger, creating the ancient imitation of today's urban legends.

We all know what can happen when things spread by word of mouth. The exaggerations grow with each repetition to the point that by the time a story reaches the tenth or fifteenth set of ears, things can be blown way out of proportion. Yet, the queen, hearing these stories of magnificence, excellence, and Solomon's wisdom, finally decided she had to see this for herself with her own eyes. She decided these tales couldn't keep coming her way by mere coincidence. It was becoming apparent it was time to make arrangements for a firsthand inspection.

In the same way now, people are saying and speaking about their experience with you and what you have to offer. There are also people who are hearing what is being said. And what those people are saying must inspire someone else enough to the point where they will spend their hard-earned resources to experience for themselves what they have heard so much about. This is the point at which we will fail or succeed. This is where people decide if it was all a bunch of hype or if the stories are for real; they will decide if it's all show and no-go, or legitimate, if we've overpromised and under-delivered. This is also time to seize upon these opportunities.

Your business or organization may not be able to offer a life-changing experience on the level of the Queen of Sheba. Still, what would happen if you tried to come close to it? You created an environment where people were honored, felt special? Whatever you did for whatever moments of time you had—you offered them a breathtaking experience? That's what this life is all about: excellence, doing the best that you possibly can with what you have been given—not so you can jump and crow and generate praise and acclaim, but so you can honor the God who created you. This is what is so rewarding about serving with excellence.

The spirit of excellence isn't reserved for those working in palaces, five-star restaurants, and executive suites. You may not have an official title, or greater responsibility than you would like right now; you may be working at a part-time minimum wage job and think no one notices you or appreciates what you do. That isn't true. The way you carry yourself and the hard work and determination in which you operate speaks volumes to people.

WHAT THE QUEEN SAW

It's worth reviewing some background of the biblical story here to get a fuller grasp on what transpired during the Queen of Sheba's visit to the royal palace in Jerusalem. Second Chronicles 9 describes how, when she saw the wisdom of Solomon and his palace, the food at his table, the seating of his servants, the service and attire of his attendants and cupbearers, and the burnt offerings he presented in the temple, it took her breath away. Today, people might ooze with comments like "#Amazing!" or "#YouGottaSeeThis!"

There are several points worth noting in what the Queen of Sheba saw:

PRINCIPLE 2: EXPERIENCE MATTERS

She saw all the wisdom of Solomon.

In Chapter Two, I mentioned how Solomon became the wisest person on Earth because he pleased God so much with his request in a dream. It is critical to this book that I note that the passage from 1 Kings 3:7–14 recounts how Solomon prayed a prayer of humility, acknowledging how God had made him king over a great nation, so great and numerous "they cannot be counted." To deal with his awesome responsibilities, he asked the Lord for an understanding heart so he could govern wisely. Pleased with Solomon's request, God replied that He would give the king wisdom like no one had ever had, as well as riches, fame, and long life.

Don't miss the key to this answered prayer. By asking for wisdom rather than riches, God granted Solomon's request to the point that he would become the wisest person who ever lived. And, because his heart was pure and he asked for the right thing, the Lord threw in riches and fame. The proof came from what the Queen of Sheba saw.

PRINCIPLE 3: DETAILS MATTER

She saw the palace he had built.

Even the architecture must have been magnificent. Every detail mattered. It's one thing to build something great, but it's another thing to maintain it. It wasn't just the architectural designs that sparkled, but the care and maintenance of those designs. Such skills had to be taught and passed on through various levels of management, cascading down to the level of the facilities engineers and groundskeepers. Solomon's vision to build and his instructions to keep the level of excellence in the upkeep of the palace—as well as the surrounding structures of the city—must have been a source of national pride. It stands to reason that Jerusalem was the cleanest city in the Middle East. It had to be to reflect the God who had directed His people there, protected them on the journey, and empowered them to take the land.

King David commissioned Solomon to build the first temple of Jerusalem. As the site for a future temple, David chose Mount Moriah, or the Temple Mount, where it was believed Abraham had built the altar on which to sacrifice his son, Isaac.[14]

This is where the level of excellence must supersede the "good enough" mindset that I mentioned in Chapter Five. It is so easy for an average kind of performance and lackluster attention to details to creep in and damage our business or organization. When we have fought for buildings and facilities and acquired (or leased) them only after great amounts of sacrifice, it is crucial to pass on the stories of what things were like when the struggles began. Rather than acting with the entitlement outlook of those who inherit what previous generations sacrificed for, the stories of what things were like in the past will help to perpetuate what we want in the present and the future.

I wonder if Solomon and his older officials recounted to the people what it was like when the Ark of the Covenant was housed in a tent rather than in the First Temple. Solomon must have told the stories. You have to share the stories of the struggle to newer hires during their orientation so they get a fuller and more comprehensive understanding of what they are a part of and the role that they play in its current and future success.

PRINCIPLE 4: PRESENTATION MATTERS

She saw the food at his table.

Since the Hebrews followed strict dietary laws, there was likely no deviation from those guidelines. No pork, clams, lobsters, or crab at the royal buffet. But the pita breads, best varieties of salads, and homemade soups would make the first course feel like the main meal. For the main course, there were likely sides of beef grilled to perfection, whole chickens baked in spices and raisins, and fresh fish from the Mediterranean steamed with curry and coriander. Plus, cakes of dates and snow from the mountains of Lebanon, brought in for real snow cones of every flavor to cleanse the palate between courses. I'm sure the feast at Solomon's table was so incredible that not only did it catch the eye of the queen, but also fulfilled any culinary desire that she had. Solomon's staff would have made sure of it.

Nor was it just the food that caught the queen's eye. It was also the presentation: the care and excellence that went into the preparation and display at the table. Eating on plates of gold and with forks, knives, and utensils of the same precious metal obviously wowed the queen. So must have the waiters, who knew from which angle they would serve various plates and which side to approach so they could cleanly remove them before the next course. They knew what tone of voice to use and proper posture. Everything was curated to perfection.

A few years ago, we had an opportunity to meet with a developer who was building a brand-new community that would contain more than three thousand homes. He had heard of our reputation for quality and wanted a face-to-face meeting with some of their staff and ours to discuss their master plan, which would include our church serving as an anchor presence in the community.

Never one to miss an opportunity to make a first impression, I suggested that we host them for lunch in our offices. Having recently completed a remodeling of our central offices, we wanted to "wow" them. During this remodeling, we had invested a substantial amount of money in our auditorium, lobby, and common areas, including our offices. I've always believed in doing the best you can with what you have, so we value-engineered everything. At the time, the economy in Hawai'i was booming, so the per-square-foot cost of remodeling had hit an all-time high. We couldn't get around that. It was time to expand, and we couldn't put off the remodeling any longer, so we did what needed to be done. (I am proud to say it made ours possibly the trendiest and coolest office structure to work at in the state.)

PRINCIPLE 5: FIRST IMPRESSIONS MATTER

She saw the seating of his servants, the attire of his attendants, cup bearers, and burnt offerings Solomon presented in the house of the Lord.

Until this point, I have conveyed a lot of the queen's experiences that had to do with food, service, and the building design of the royal palace and the First Temple. But no matter how beautiful a building is and how well-planned everything is, thanks to skilled interior designers and architects, it still has no heart. The heart and essence of anything that is built has everything to do with the people whom you do it with and those you serve. The queen encountered the excellence of the staff. Meticulously trained and carefully selected, only the "best of the best" would have been allowed to interact with Solomon's guests and the queen's entourage. It must have been such an incredible honor! The people whom the queen encountered on her visit left an indelible mark.

When we hosted the first potential developer of our building, we treated two of their top staff members by ordering some great food from a premiere caterer, presenting them in chafing dishes so our guests could serve themselves, buffet style. Needless to say, it was a major win. They told us that we were not like any other churches or pastors they had spoken to or met with. The interior design of our new offices blew them away; they were almost dumbfounded by the entire experience. After dessert, we gave them a tour of the rest of the building and won them over.

Unfortunately, after eighteen months of planning, negotiations, and building trust, this developer decided to scrap the whole concept. After he returned our deposit, we were left in a lurch—or so we thought. Within forty-eight hours, a second developer contacted us. Now, we had met previously with this company a couple times but on neutral turf. The president wanted to visit our offices and tour the facilities to get an up-close look at our operation and discuss an arrangement similar to the first developer's proposal.

Since I had important business on the mainland, I wasn't present for this site visit. However, because I had prepared our team to handle the responsibilities of such an important occasion, they knew all the protocols. Especially the standard that whenever someone new is being introduced in the office that they are to stop work, stand up, and come to introduce themselves as they greet a guest warmly. That's exactly what happened. (I asked for a verbal report immediately after the meeting.)

The spirit of our team and the excellence of our building moved this particular developer to the point of tears. We literally took her breath away! At one point, an aide told me that the developer stood there speechless. Of course, I know it was the culture of our staff and the special environment, but I also believe we over-delivered on the expectations of what a church looks like and how its people operate. To repeat the title of Ritz-Carlton hotel cofounder Horst Schulze's book, *Excellence Wins*. This led to a partnership with her company; in the first quarter of 2021 we were preparing to build a new sanctuary and offices after purchasing three acres in this development (on some of the state's most expensive property).

PRINCIPLE 6: YOUR SYSTEMS & STRUCTURES MATTER

She saw the organization of his officials.

By seeing the way his officials sat, the queen developed an appreciation for the order and careful organization at the place. It offered a visual picture of Solomon's organizational chart. She could tell who oversaw which departments and who reported to whom. Having a keen administrative mind, her team likely asked for job descriptions and organizational charts and requested how-to manuals and recipes from the royal kitchen to accentuate what she had in the Kingdom of Sheba.

PRINCIPLE 7: STYLE MATTERS

She saw the way that they were clothed.

There is no way getting around this: Solomon's staff was out to make first and lasting impressions. So, they wore impressive attire and clothing. Taking note of this, the queen endeavored to creatively adapt everything she saw into the context of her kingdom.

The First Temple King Solomon built stood for nearly 400 years.

Now, you may not have a lot of money to buy expensive, tailored clothing, but it doesn't take a fortune to look sharp, turn heads, and make an impression. It's all about the presentation, which has a lot to do with the care and pride you take in your appearance. At work, simply be well-groomed and wear pressed or steamed outfits, wrinkle-free and fresh-looking. If your job requires makeup, then do a good job at it; get up earlier to give yourself time. Don't allow yourself to look hurried or harried. This means doing the best you can with what you have. Growing up and being on a tight budget—even into the early years of marriage—I learned to pinch pennies while still taking pride in my appearance. Yes, I know, the Bible says man looks at the outward appearance but God looks at the heart. However, people may never get a chance to know your heart as well if you don't make a lasting impression on them in what you say, how you look, and what you do.

PRINCIPLE 8: EXCELLENCE MATTERS

She saw his cupbearers.

In the ancient world, cupbearers were some of the most important people in a kingdom. Cupbearers to a king could have no ulterior motives or agendas. They had to have the perfect reputation, disposition, and personality for the job. Carefully selected and trained over the years, cupbearers would be privy to private conversations and considered advisers to royalty, in addition to being the taste-testers of everything the king, queen, and other members of the royal family ate or drank. I'm sure they had to approve of the taste, but they also needed to be the first line of defense for the safety of the monarchy. This was a very tight circle. One of the most famous cupbearers in the Old Testament was Nehemiah, who served King Artaxerxes in Persia. Because of Nehemiah's impeccable reputation, the king granted his request to return to Jerusalem to rebuild its walls and gates, more than 140 years after it fell to the Babylonians (long after Solomon's reign).

THE ONE HONORED

The most important thing to remember here is that she heard of Solomon's fame that brought honor to the name of the Lord, as outlined in 1 Kings 10. The first two verses tell about the queen coming to test Solomon with questions, arriving with a large group of attendants and a great caravan, loaded with a small fortune in spices, gold, and precious jewels. Even a rapper would have been impressed.

For the queen, a journey to Jerusalem meant considerable planning and logistics. She would have to travel by caravan for more than 1,500 miles—just over half the distance between Los Angeles and New York! Passing through such modern-day countries as Sudan and Egypt, she possibly could have crossed the Red Sea, gone through Yemen and into Saudi Arabia, then on to Israel, and finally into Jerusalem.

She brought with her as a gift to Solomon the largest quantity of spices and jewels that had ever been given, plus great quantities of gold. (As I noted in the introduction, the gold alone was worth more than $285 million!) The caravan she traveled with would definitely have had soldiers to protect her, positioned at the front and at the back of the entourage to protect the queen and their precious cargo. Today, funds can be wired across the globe electronically in a matter of mere seconds. Back then, they had to be pulled on carts by beasts of burden. Remember, the queen was bringing gifts to Solomon out of her abundance and wealth. She was already accustomed to a high level of luxury and opulence. Yet, despite being a monarch and coming from a great dynasty, the queen was about to encounter something greater than she had ever experienced. She would be forever changed.

CHALLENGING THE STATUS QUO

Because of everything she saw, heard, and felt, the Queen of Sheba was blown away. Solomon's wisdom, the city of Jerusalem and its magnificent buildings, and the excellence of the palace staff made for an incredible, life-changing encounter. She had heard it all back at home, but now she saw it all. It was an *experience* for her and her entourage. Like the queen, her servants and the members of her traveling party would never forget what they saw. After they saw what they did in Jerusalem, they knew it was well worth the trip.

During the days that followed, they would soak up what they had experienced. This would not be tossed away as just another royal visit that was one for the books. There would be expectations before they arrived back in Sheba. They would likely debrief all the way back home from Jerusalem. The scribes would take notes and add personal observations as everyone reflected on changes they needed to make. Most would be excited; others were likely nervous. Their comfort in the status quo had been challenged. They could expect the queen to want to take things to the next level in hospitality, service, and standards of excellence. Excellence had just been redefined—right before their very eyes.

part three

07: Build To Change

08: Build To Last

09: Build To Leave A Legacy

10: Keep Enterprising If You Want To Keep Rising

FINISH BETTER: CULTIVATING A LEGACY

BUILD TO CHANGE

How you begin an endeavor will often determine how long you last—if you last.

07

Group A	Group B
The New England Patriots	The Kansas City Chiefs
The San Antonio Spurs	The Los Angeles Lakers
The taxi industry	Uber
Sports Authority	Dick's Sporting Goods
Countrywide Home Loans	Rocket Mortgages
Blockbuster Video	Netflix

Most everyone recognizes the names listed above in Group A and their fading fortunes, compared to the success stories of those in Group B. The first list represents examples of companies that didn't turn the corner to survive into the 2020s and beyond. Or, in the case of football's Patriots and basketball's Spurs, lost their places of prominence in their respective professional sports. We could add to these more well-known names many lower-profile businesses, organizations, and churches that didn't prepare to innovate prior to COVID-19. These are all examples of cautionary tales of the famous Bell Curve, otherwise known as the Sigmoid Curve. But more on that later.

After the 2020 season, the New England Patriots missed the playoffs for the first time in a dozen years, a stunning reversal after nineteen straight winning seasons, seventeen playoff appearances, nine Super Bowl appearances, and six Vince Lombardi championship *trophies since Bill Belichick took over as head coach in 2000.[15] Yet we saw a hint of the team's downfall in the reportedly rocky relationship between Belichick and star quarterback Tom Brady near the end of Brady's concurrent stay in New England. Brady went on to sign a free agent contract with the Tampa Bay Bucs and lead the team to its first Super Bowl in nearly two decades.*

The Patriots' demise parallels the end of the dynasty of the San Antonio Spurs after the Spurs were labeled the "gold standard" of sports franchises. That reputation stemmed from its sustained success, which many credited to a culture that bred championships. Gregg Popovich—who entered the 2020-21 season as the longest-tenured coach in major sports leagues—coached the Spurs to five championships in twenty-two seasons. And, made the playoffs for a record twenty-two consecutive seasons! This franchise is to be admired and appreciated; it will always be considered one of the tops in all sports.

However, that came to an end in 2020. In 2018, San Antonio had its culture tested when star player Kawhi Leonard forced a trade to the Toronto Raptors. In return, the Spurs didn't obtain enough value for him for them to remain competitive. Part of the problem: They relied on their "big three" players (Manu Ginobili, Tony Parker, and Tim Duncan), for short-term success to keep the dynasty going, while not restocking the shelves in preparation for these iconic players' retirements. So, when Leonard demanded to be traded, the team didn't have the talent to sustain its winning culture.

HOW THINGS CHANGE

Such falls from the pinnacle of success remind me of a passage in famed writer Ernest Hemingway's debut novel, *The Sun Also Rises*. A character named Mike is asked how he fell into bankruptcy. Reflecting, Mike replies, "Two ways . . . gradually, then suddenly." What insight! Decline occurs almost imperceptibly at first, with small wrinkles giving signs of trouble, until they gather enough steam that they roll downhill with nothing to halt their progress.

This wasn't the story when the Queen of Sheba arrived in Jerusalem, though. What she saw was something akin to the Patriots, the Spurs, and the All Blacks (whom I mentioned in Chapter Five) in their heydays: a man at the top of his game, guiding a powerful nation and sitting on top of the world. First Kings 10:6–9 outlines the specifics as it recalls the queen exclaiming to King Solomon how everything she had heard about his achievements and wisdom was true. Her words flowed with more enthusiasm and emotion than the longest speech ever offered at an Academy Awards ceremony.

In fact, she gushed, and she hadn't even heard half the story of his greatness. His wisdom and prosperity were beyond his reputation, so much so that his officials must have been privileged to stand in his presence each day, soaking up his wisdom.

She praised the God who had placed him on the throne, saying His eternal love for Israel had led Him to make Solomon king.

Historically, it is reported that King Solomon became richer and wiser than any king on earth.

A recent *National Geographic* series about the history of the Bible points out how it depicts Solomon's reign as an era of unprecedented prosperity because of the wisdom God bestowed on him. Among the steps the magazine said Solomon took were reorganizing the nation into a dozen districts that cut across tribal boundaries and centralized power in Jerusalem. While not necessarily an admirable step, Solomon continued his father's policy of taking wives from various tribes to pacify tribal sensibilities—and from other nations with whom Solomon formed alliances.

> *"The Bible says that Israel grew prosperous under Solomon, and indeed there is evidence that the Levant was experiencing strong economic growth as regional trade increased in the region," writes Jean-Pierre Isbouts. "Wealth poured into his treasury, allowing Solomon to fulfill God's promise to David: to build a temple to house the Ark of the Covenant. To do so, he launched a 'donation drive' that netted 5,000 gold and 10,000 silver talents (roughly $100 million in today's currency). When the project was finished, a citadel of white and gold had risen over Jerusalem. The Temple built by Solomon would become the spiritual center of Jerusalem."*[16]

You can see why monarchs and dignitaries came from far and wide, and from multiple nations, to consult with the king and to hear the wisdom he would espouse from his enormous throne. Year after year everyone who visited him brought gifts of silver and gold, clothing, weapons, spices, horses, and mules. In fact, silver became so plentiful throughout the kingdom, Solomon made it as common as ordinary cobblestones. When it comes to impressive feats in your business or organizational endeavors, try duplicating that one.

As 1 Kings outlines, the excellence the Queen of Sheba experienced took her breath away, leaving her at a loss for words. When she arrived in Jerusalem, she stepped into a culture of excellence that had already been created and curated for years. She had not seen what it took to build what Solomon had established, but any leader at that level has to admire the tremendous effort that must have required. As such, she hadn't not just "heard the half of it." Nor did she know about the first half, or the twenty years it took to build. But there is a second half we will also find intriguing.

Solomon reigned approximately forty years as king during the highest, most prosperous period in Israel's history. Many referred to the first half as "The Golden Age" for Israel. Then there was the second half, where Solomon took his eyes off the prize. In his book, *How the Mighty Fall,* Jim Collins observes: "Every company and institution, no matter how great, is vulnerable to decline."[17] The other half that the queen would not see was the last half of Solomon's reign and its aftermath. After

Solomon's death, Israel would plunge into a decline spiritually, morally, and then economically. In fact, cracks had already been appearing in the foundation.

It is estimated the three thousand talents of gold and seven thousand talents of silver King David, Solomon's father, gave to build the temple would be roughly worth about $867.5 million today.[18]

At the end of the slide, the grandeur and glory of Israel, a special nation composed of God's chosen people, would be ripped apart and separated into two different kingdoms under the leadership of Solomon's son, Rehoboam. This descent would ultimately mar Solomon's standing in history, damaging his legacy and casting doubt on his wisdom. Near the end of his life, he would call all worldly achievements, riches, and other trophies people often esteem "vanity."

If wisdom builds a house, then a lack of wisdom can tear it down. If excellence and great customer service can build a brand, then forsaking those values can bring it to an abrupt halt. Solomon was the wisest man on earth, but wisdom is only as good as long as it is applied. As my good friend and mentor, Dr. Sam Chand, says in his book *Bigger, Faster Leadership*: "A lifecycle of organizations is true and in this exact order for businesses, churches, shopping malls, neighborhoods, marriages, and every other type of human enterprise."[19]

FIVE ORGANIZATIONAL PHASES

The kingdom Solomon built went through five different phases. Apply this to any area of your life, business, or organization, and I'm sure you'll be able to identify where you are. Outlined by Dr. Chand, they include:

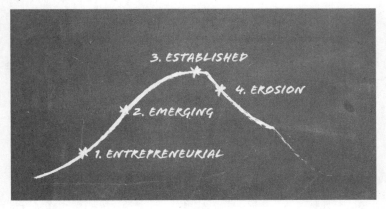

1) "The *entrepreneurial* (discovery) phase is the exciting beginning, when every dream seems possible. It includes the culture creating and curating phases of the kingdom. This is where the hustle and grit of the owner/leader

leverages their time and effort. This is the fun part. Roots are going deep, and long hours are applied. This is especially true for those who are launching businesses.

2) "The *emerging* (growth) phase is when the vision begins to take definite shape, leaders are empowered, and the organization sees real progress. In this phase, this is where we are in search of leaders/organizations that we can 'draft' the way a long-distance runner does behind someone in the lead. These people or organizations serve as *pacesetters* as we look to track and emulate either their model and/or their methods. Creative adaptation takes place through traveling to a destination where the headquarters is located for an on-site visit, ala the Queen of Sheba.

3) "The *established* (maintenance) phase is a time when leaders take a deep breath, enjoy their success, and watch their systems function well. But this phase is also dangerous because it can easily lead to complacency. This becomes the most critical phase for leaders of organizations who feel as though they have 'arrived.' This is where the temptation to kick back and enjoy the fruits of their labors kick in and motivation begins to wane.

4) "The *erosion* (survival) phase is evident when the organization shows signs of decline, and the earlier vision seems unreachable. This is the phase where, slowly, things begin to be chipped away. It starts first with a trickle. People start leaving the staff; they begin looking for other places

to work because they are either disenfranchised or disillusioned with the culture.

5) "The *enterprising* (reinvention) phase is the result of a deeper grasp of the need, a renewed vision, fresh enthusiasm, and new strategies to meet the need. Giving an existing organization a fresh charge of vision and energy is difficult, but it's essential for future flourishing."[20]

Parts one and two of this book covered the entrepreneurial, emerging, and established phases. Looking at the graphic, you will see all the phases applied to the Sigmoid/bell curve.

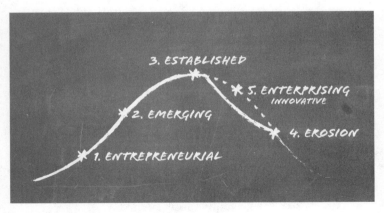

LAUNCHING AN ENDEAVOR

How you begin an endeavor will often determine how long you last—if you last. This is true in so many areas of life, whether that involves marriage, other important relationships, or business. So, the *entrepreneurial* phase is critical to your start. But equally important is the *emerging* phase. You are familiar with the old saying, "character counts." And it truly does. Because hindsight is 20/20, we could always look back and find examples of where some of the best and the brightest began to give off clues of what their future would look like.

But the next two phases are critical to any business or organization at any level if it hopes to create sustainability that continues to grow "up and to the right of the chart." We all want our excellence, customer service, the creating of a great culture, and creative adaptation to take us further than we ever imagined. Many of us would like to see it handed off to someone else who deserves it. Or, at the very least, that will appreciate it and value what has been accomplished.

Now, nobody intends to start something worthwhile, build it to a level of satisfaction while they pour their lives into a great work, and then see it fizzle. Everyone has dreams of possibly handing it off to family members or transitioning it to another president, CEO, or capable manager who can continue to carry the torch. No one intends to fail in the middle phase of organizational building or watch it fail as they near the end of their career. Yet sometimes it happens. I believe there are *three main sources* with the potential to stop every organization from growing and propel it down the slow slide into decline. I'm sure that there are more, but here are three I have identified:

1) *Losing the Mission*: Often referred to as "mission drift," this occurs when your business or organization starts to move away from its original, intended purpose and its mission statement. In most cases, this happens by accident.

That's why a clear, concise mission statement helps everyone to stay on track. Sometimes, mission statements need periodic curating, to see if either the mission remains the same or if it needs to be changed and adjusted.

The architectural design of the First Temple was modeled after the tabernacle that had housed the Ark of the Covenant for decades (if not centuries). Quite lavish, it was double the size and built mainly from stone, with cedar paneling to hide all masonry, which was overlaid with gold.[21]

2) *The Leadership*: Often there's nothing wrong with the mission; leadership falls short. Major sports franchises are often scrutinized and applauded for great ownership, including the general manager, head coach, staff, and players. Or, they are criticized for falling short, be that erratic decision-making, pulling the trigger too quickly with coaches after a losing season or two, or squabbling and dysfunction whose impact can be felt throughout the building. Every franchise wants to win a championship, but the difference-maker is how they

go about the mission. If a franchise is not aligned in any one of these key areas, the playoffs could be a possibility, but a championship is not likely. In the same way, a business could have well-intentioned owners and attract young talent, but if the managers don't have what it takes to lead well, there are bound to be problems. Sometimes, leadership does not have the capacity, the skill, or the know-how to grow with the company to the next level. That requires some tough decisions, be that lateral movements (shifting people to different departments according to their skill and experience), demotions, or even helping some folks refuel and move on to a new career.

3) *Systems and Structures*: As Dr. Sam Chand writes, "The acceleration of your growth is contingent on the excellence of your systems and your structures."[22] I have personally observed churches, businesses, and organizations that did not scale their business plan properly, or they grew so rapidly that they could not keep up with their growth. As a result, compromises in their culture and weaknesses in their leadership inevitably began to show, and cracks in the foundation began to spread.

THE NEED FOR AGILITY

There is well-documented evidence of businesses that never made the necessary adjustments and thus were never able to creatively adapt to new dilemmas. When it comes to technological advancements, global economic demands, or just the simple conveniences and preferences of a tech-savvy generation, agility and pivoting (the hot words of COVID-19 business jargon) are critical to survival.

If this was true during the pre-pandemic era, it proved even more so during COVID-19—and the years leading up to it. Why Blockbuster went out of business is a harrowing tale of missed opportunity and settling for "good enough." In the late 1990s, when Marc Rudolph received a charge for a $40 late fee from Blockbuster, he knew there had to be a more efficient and effective way to rent movies without penalizing customers. Ultimately, this is what birthed the idea for Netflix, which started by mailing DVDs to subscribers and allowing them to keep a certain number without late fees, before later moving to its digital subscription streaming service in 2007. (Ironically, about three million customers still opt for getting movies by mail instead of downloading them.)

However, Netflix was still in its relevant infancy when a new business partner, Netflix's current CEO Reed Hastings, and several others secured more backing from business investors. Eventually, Netflix gained enough traction to pitch a sale of the company to one of the largest home video and video game rental businesses: Blockbuster. The only problem came when Blockbuster's CEO, John Antioco, laughed at their proposal to acquire Netflix for $50 million.

In 2000, John Antioco saw no need for Netflix's ideas. After all, Blockbuster made almost sixteen percent of its revenues from late fees alone. Fast forward a decade and Blockbuster was filing for bankruptcy. In 2014, the once-dominant rental chain closed its last corporate-owned store. Now, only one store remains in Bend, Oregon, a nostalgic, popular tourist destination for what once was. Talk about too little too late! Blockbuster's failure to move past good enough ultimately cost it a doorway into a $20-billion industry while spelling its inevitable demise.

Blockbuster experienced massive erosion because its leadership was not agile and creative enough to adapt their mission. They were blinded by their dominance of the market and stuck in an old model of VHS tapes, Blu-ray discs, and DVDs. They were also stuck in a system and structure that demanded real estate, more employees, and high-end retail leases at hundreds of stores. Because they could not see the emergence of downloadable streaming content, they missed their golden opportunity. They didn't anticipate what this current world that you and I live in would look like—all because they were enticed by the late fees that made them so much money. Netflix said, "Who cares about late fees?"

Look at Netflix today. Its third quarter revenues in 2020 totaled more than $6.4 billion, compared to $5.2 billion for the third quarter of the previous year. Annual revenues for 2019 were approximately $20.2 billion, more than triple Blockbuster's best year (2004), when its revenue amounted to $5.9 billion. I should add that other more creative companies came into this space, especially Redbox with its video-rental kiosks. When still publicly held, the company reported annual revenue of $2 billion for 2016. The moral of the story is how the mighty can fall!

DANGER OF PRIDE

After experiencing great success, every one of us, including our businesses and organizations, are vulnerable to what Jim Collins terms *hubris*; the Bible calls it *pride*. One way organizations succumb to this disease is becoming so successful that they run the risk of becoming overconfident, bordering on the verge of arrogance. This can flow into mission drift and not caring about who got you where you are, forgetting about where you came from, and not caring about how you can still get there.

Pride comes before a hard, concrete landing. The reality of that fall is often public and quite painful. Just because you can do something doesn't mean you should. One of the signs of hubris in companies and organizations is when they lose their focus on their mission and begin to expand resources in areas that do not complement their long-term goals and mission. They take their eyes off the prize and place them on ancillary pet projects—just because they can. I've seen it happen so many times in the sphere of influence where I live. As a result, I'm very aware of the potential for our organization to fall into the same trap.

The next chapter will address the phase we are all attempting to avoid. To build like Solomon is one thing; building a business, church, or organization to the point where success brings fans, followers, customers and clients . . . isn't that one of the goals? And to have people experience what you've contributed to; wouldn't that be rewarding? Yes and yes! However, to do all of that is one thing. But to build something that lasts, has sustainability, longevity, and leaves a legacy—that's another. In fact, it's the *main thing*.

BUILD TO LAST

Everybody needs a coach or consultant in their lives.

08

At home here in the Hawaiian Islands, we have three mountain peaks that periodically get snow between the months of November and March. I know for some of you it may be hard to believe, but it does sometimes snow in paradise. Yet until a recent vacation trip—that, among other places, took us through Arizona—I didn't know a basic truth about snow. I made this discovery during a vacation to visit members of my extended family at the end of 2020 and beginning of 2021.

One of the greatest things about this trip was not just reconnecting with my parents, my siblings, and various nieces and nephews. We also got to travel to the Grand Canyon. Considered one of the seven natural wonders of the world, this awesome slice of creation stretches for 227 miles and averages over ten miles in width. (Just hiking across that span might take me a couple days, given the rugged terrain). As soon as we arrived, I could see why this national park is such a popular destination for hiking, rafting, camping, climbing, and sightseeing. I had only seen its splendor on television or travelogues, never experiencing it in person. So, you can imagine the excitement and anticipation coursing through my veins when we reached the edge of the canyon.

What made it extra special, though, was that it snowed the day we arrived at the Grand Canyon and at the most populated town nearby—Flagstaff, Arizona, a city of seventy-two thousand. Although it snowed for only two days, on our final day in the state while *driving three hours back to Phoenix to catch our flight, I noticed something that a typical Hawaiian would not have firsthand knowledge of. Namely, that snow melts at the edges. Now this might not be brand new information for some of you, but it often begins on the outside. As the day grows warmer, it eventually makes its way until it melts at the core. It doesn't melt from the middle and work its way toward the outside.*

That's just like culture erosion. Things start to slowly erode on the edges, but only after years of undetected root problems, issues, or areas that are left unaddressed. Eventually, it can lead to the worst-case scenario: an avalanche. It doesn't happen overnight. It can take months or even years, but when it happens, it seems like it happened almost overnight. Yet, it didn't. The signs were there for a long time, as we will see with Solomon.

DISTURBING TRENDS

There were disturbing trends with the wisest, richest, and most powerful ruler in Israel's history. As so often happens with megawatt personalities whose influence grows to mammoth proportions, many of their aides and followers are afraid to say anything—sometimes because they know they are putting their livelihood at risk. The cautions raised by those who are brave enough to speak are either ignored or dismissed with the wave of a hand and a snide remark that the person is a troublemaker or malcontent. While the exact details of what happened at the palace aren't known, the signs became clear. I have identified five lessons from the end of Solomon's life that, if heeded, can help you not lose it all:

1. STICK TO YOUR CORE VALUES

As goes the leader, eventually so goes the organization. And almost always, eventually everything. While it was published back in early 2014, the book *Mission Drift* still generates considerable attention in organizational circles. Co-authors Peter Greer and Chris Horst are executives with a microfinance non-profit; their findings apply to businesses, organizations, and churches alike.

They coined the term "Mission True" to denote those organizations that remain faithful to their founder's vision and carry out that mission, writing: "Mission True organizations know why they exist and protect their core at all costs. They remain faithful to what they believe God has entrusted them to do.

They define what is immutable: their values and purposes, their DNA, their heart and soul."[23]

According to Greer and Horst, it is not uncommon for the founders of an organization to be crystal clear on their mission and purpose. But it is often when subsequent generations take over that the original, intended mission of the organization goes so far off course that it no longer resembles what the founder had in mind. Over time, as new leaders assume control of the organization, changes are made that threaten the mission.

Among the examples the authors list: Harvard University, which originally only employed Christian professors; the Pew Charitable Trusts, which now funds causes that patriarch Howard Pew (a strong Christian) would never have approved of; and the organization formerly known as the YMCA (for Young Men's Christian Organization).

Let's explore the latter: In 1844, George Williams, a farmer turned department store worker, was troubled by the conditions he observed in industrialized London, especially for young men who had migrated to the city from rural areas to find jobs. Although just twenty-two years old, Williams joined eleven friends to organize the first YMCA as a refuge of Bible study and prayer for those wanting to escape the hazards of London's street life.

Becoming a worldwide organization now based in Geneva, Switzerland, the YMCA aimed to put Christian principles into practice by developing a healthy "body, mind, and spirit." Although I had a membership to my local YMCA, primarily so I could play basketball there twice a week, COVID-19 and social distancing brought that to a halt. I had to find other places to play and in recent months even started playing pickleball, a paddleball sport that combines elements of badminton, tennis, and ping-pong; it is reportedly the nation's fastest-growing sport.[24]

But my point isn't about pickleball or basketball—it's how badly the YMCA has drifted from its mission. Started as a specifically Christian-based endeavor, the YMCA eventually trained and commissioned more than twenty thousand missionaries. Yet, as the organization grew and expanded to multiple countries, its focus drifted increasingly towards health and fitness, with little reference to the original mission. Many locations became more like community centers, offering a series of special-interest classes and exercise sessions, and at the same time embracing a polytheistic culture. By 2010, the YMCA had dropped three of its four letters to simply be called the Y, removing any remaining ties to its original Christian mission.

In an interview about *Mission Drift*, Greer talked about how incremental shifts can occur when a group appoints board members whose values aren't in sync with the organization's mission: "The more we researched, the more we realized that it's not like one major event. There's not one major decision [that takes the organization off its Christian mission] . . . It's all these really small decisions and you don't really see the impact until you take a step back and see the difference that time allows and perspective . . . We found that 'mission drift' often starts with boards. As much intentionality as there is around hiring staff, often times there's not that same type of process and scrutiny and understanding with whom you invite on your board."[25]

If a business or organization can lose its original mission and values, then it is highly possible that it starts with the leadership that comes after the leader. I would venture to guess that the subsequent leaders after Sir George Williams did not carry the same values that he lived by. And herein lies the problem with Solomon. Solomon drifted away from his core values.

The construction of Solomon's Temple took seven years.[26]

2. BRIDLE YOUR PASSIONS

Having an excess of resources is not necessarily a bad thing, but what you do with the excess can determine the course of your organization. While Solomon saw himself as invincible, the excesses of life that he participated in trying to fulfill every desire of his heart would play a role in his downfall. Solomon was an "all-in" type of guy. If he needed a wife, Solomon didn't stop at one; he had more than seven hundred! And, if they weren't enough, he added another three hundred concubines (at one per day, it would take almost three years to spend one night with each woman). Let that reality sink in for a moment. Can you imagine what the weekly spa and food bill looked like? Literally insane. If Solomon wanted to mount up on a horse and go for a ride that day, no problem, pick any one out of the 12,000 steeds available. Or if he wanted to get some work done that day, but needed to visit one of his other palaces or review his troops, say no more—he had 1,400 homes. To be fair, most of the horses and chariots were likely prepared for battle, if and when the time came to protect their borders. But you get the idea.

So, while Solomon built an incredible kingdom and possessed more wisdom than anyone else on earth, he never learned to control his unbridled passions. With gold hovering just over $1,850 an ounce in early 2021, his annual haul of twenty-five tons of gold meant Solomon netted the modern-day equivalent of more than $59 million a year, every year. Not to mention his fleet of oceangoing ships, with riches flowing to Jerusalem through commerce, trading, gifts, tribute money, and taxation.

However, he was also the epitome of a man who had it all and who eventually lost it all. (Remember, as goes the leader, so goes the organization.) In the final years of his life, Solomon would write the book of Ecclesiastes. In it, he laments the vanity of life and how he chased after everything imaginable, only to discover utter emptiness. He would lament the pleasure that he sought, the overindulgence of wine that he consumed, the huge and beautiful homes that he built, the vineyards that he planted, the gardens and parks that he created, the slaves that he bought, and the great sums of silver, gold, and other treasures he accumulated.

The end result sounds like a plaintive cry of regret and dismay. In Ecclesiastes 2:10–11, Solomon laments how he took anything and everything he wanted while never denying himself a single pleasure; he even enjoyed hard work. But later, when he looked back at all his labors and all he had accomplished, he said it was like chasing the wind. In the end, he called it all meaningless. How sad.

3. GET A COACH OR CONSULTANT

Everybody needs a coach or consultant in their lives. I'm blessed to have a few of them speaking into different areas of my life. In order for you and your organization to succeed, you need the right people with the right skill set and expertise to speak into your life. Think about it: A personal trainer must be at the top of their game when it comes to nutrition, as well as at their peak physically. Nobody hires an out-of-shape personal trainer. They will first lose credibility and eventually clients. Nobody would hire a broke financial planner or a life insurance salesman who didn't own any policies offered by their company. Additionally, police officers must obey the laws of the land and pastors must practice what they preach. Not only is consistency important, so is allowing others around us to point out when we fail to live by the values we espouse.

Here in Hawai'i, there is a humorous, common saying, "Never trust a skinny chef." Why? Because he's probably not eating his own cooking! In the same way, Solomon was great at dispensing wisdom but failed to follow his own advice. Instead of surrounding himself with a multitude of counselors, consultants, or coaches (even though he penned great advice in Proverbs about the safety for a nation that originates with many advisers), he was too wise in his own eyes. The wisest man on earth never applied the wisdom he had gained. Consider that:

» Solomon was unteachable.

As the wisest man on earth, he thought nobody could teach him anything he didn't already know. By the time he was a young adult, Solomon had likely outgrown all his mentors and was trying to forget what everybody else was just starting to learn. We could compare him to a fourteen-year-old child prodigy who is already studying for an MBA at Harvard, doing a residency at John Hopkins at sixteen, and performing brain surgery at eighteen. Who teaches the ultimate teacher? Nobody. Well, that's what many brilliant people think, while forgetting the credit ultimately goes to the Creator who gave them their talents. A couple years ago I saw an article in a national magazine where the author noted that while Solomon had much wisdom, he forgot who gave it to him; as a result he allowed his opinion of self to be elevated beyond reason.

» Solomon was unleadable.

Although people may make it to the top of their field, some may even grace the cover of national magazines, and see their names become verbs in popular culture, time and pressure will be the proof of that sustainability. But if we have no coaches or mentors, if we are not leadable and accountable, all the fame and influence in the world will prove to be futile. If pride comes before a fall, then narcissism is a close second.

Over the years, I have seen many in my field of work fall from grace. Mostly men, although some women too, who attained it all and eventually lost it all. Their boards have been rendered powerless and their advisors have given up trying to advise them. They surrounded themselves with people who only agreed with them and provided an echo chamber, with no one ever letting them know that "the emperor has no clothes." Eventually, the naked ruler's foibles are exposed, and there goes everything that was hard earned. It is no longer *erosion*; it's an all-out avalanche.

» Solomon was untouchable.

If you are extremely successful, but you are unteachable and unleadable, then sadly, your success will be short-lived. Please understand, I am literally writing this for myself, right now! And, I'm not even placing myself in that "category" of rarefied air! Because Solomon was considered—in today's vernacular—a "unicorn," nobody could touch him. It's likely the only person with the authority and credentials to confront him would have been his father, but David was dead.

When he was alive, the great thing about David was he had several prophets in his life who confronted him in key moments in his leadership, particularly the prophet, Nathan. Though he could have lost his head for it, Nathan called David out for his murderous affair with Bathsheba. There were other times when these prophets would encourage him. Such moments proved invaluable to David and his kingdom. Whenever we read about Solomon, we never hear about a prophet who was invited to speak into his life. He had no counselors, coaches, or consultants around him. When you think about it, it's a failure of epic proportions.

The First Temple contained five altars: one at the entrance of the Holy of Holies, two others within the building, a large bronze one before the porch, and a large, tiered altar in the courtyard. A huge bronze bowl, or "sea," in the courtyard was used for the priests' ablutions. Within the Holy of Holies, two cherubim of olive wood stood with the Ark; this innermost sanctuary was considered the dwelling place of God and could be entered only by the high priest and only on the Day of Atonement.[27]

4. SEE PEOPLE AS JEWELS, NOT TOOLS

The Bible says Solomon overtaxed his kingdom. In other words, he overtaxed his people and placed heavier burdens on them than were necessary. These were the people that planted the gardens, oversaw the construction of his building projects, worked in his vineyards, and fought in his military. Whenever a government over-taxes its people for the sake of supporting a bloated bureaucracy and governmental institutions, it leaves less money in the pockets of the people with which to build a life. In Israel, it likely stifled creativity and ingenuity while lowering the levels of self-determination that existed, even in a kingdom where people were subject to an all-powerful king. This hindered entrepreneurial leanings; it's as if people stopped growing because they were so dependent on the kingdom for survival. They wound up giving so much effort to supporting the kingdom, they had nothing left.

In the same way in a modern business, corporation, or other organizations, whenever people feel underappreciated and groan under the unreasonable demands placed on them, it is cause for greater employee turnover. Retaining qualified employees and attracting new talent becomes increasingly harder to accomplish, leaving the company ripe for a nasty internal split, a corporate takeover, or various groups of dissatisfied employees branching off to go do their own thing because *anything would be better than this*.

In the classic fable by Aesop, "The Scorpion and the Frog," a scorpion asks a frog to carry him over a river. The frog is afraid of being stung, but the scorpion argues that if it did so, both would sink and the scorpion would drown. The frog then agrees, but midway across the river the scorpion does indeed sting the frog, dooming them both. When asked why, the scorpion points out, "I couldn't help it. It's in my nature." In Israel, the kingdom's subjects—the people who got him across the river—were the frog and the king was the scorpion. Stinging the people upset the entire future of Israel. Everything went downhill from there.

5. KEEP GOOD MARGINS IN YOUR LIFE

Margins are like guardrails. They keep you from falling off the cliff! It's hard to imagine the obligations Solomon piled up in his quest for more and more. Things like all the palaces, the temple, the Hall of Pillars, the Hall of Justice, the fleet of ships and all the harbors they required, and all the stables for his thousands of horses and chariots. Then there were the two hundred large shields made of hammered gold, weighing at least fifteen pounds each; another three hundred smaller shields of gold weighing nearly four pounds apiece; and Solomon's huge throne, decorated with ivory and overlaid with fine gold. Plus, the shrines that he built to please his wives (who prayed to different gods than his). All these projects put a great strain on the economy of Israel. They proved to be difficult to financially sustain, which is why taxes increased and the people groaned.

If you remember nothing else about Solomon's demise, remember this: *Just because you can, it doesn't mean that you should.* Companies that expand too quickly, churches that build too soon, and entrepreneurs who are eager to take advantage of opportunity without realistically scaling their business—we are all susceptible to making such errors. How the wisest man in the world could not balance his budget, I do not know. But this much I do know: We would do well to learn from the latter half of Solomon's life, so that we can build to last and ultimately, finish better.

BUILD TO LEAVE A LEGACY

Enterprise takes vision to see
what no one else sees.

09

As you know from my account in Chapter Three of repeatedly watching The Last Dance on ESPN, I'm a huge basketball fan. I love playing the game whenever I can. Growing up, I always looked forward to my first pair of shoes to start the season. My younger brother was an All-State basketball player in Hawai'i, and I took pride in treating him to a new pair of shoes at the beginning of every season. In my family, it is a true statement when we say, "Ball is life."

I also played baseball and my shoe brand of choice, from T-ball to my days in Senior Little League, was Puma. Back in the mid- to late 1970s, we didn't have a lot of choices of retailers when it came to sports equipment. I grew up in the little sugar plantation town of Honoka'a on the Big Island of Hawai'i, and the nearest retailer was in a neighboring town fifteen miles away. (We were deprived big time compared to kids today.)

However, I soon moved on from Puma to other brands that hit the market by the time I started playing high school sports. New brands like Nike, Converse, and Adidas entered the marketplace to compete with established brands like Etonic, Pony, and Puma. The latter trio were quickly losing popularity among the coveted demographic of athletic shoe connoisseurs of the day.

A DIFFERENT DIRECTION

Everything changed in the shoe world in 1984 when Nike signed rookie phenom Michael Jordan of the Chicago Bulls to a groundbreaking shoe deal that gave us the release of the prized Air Force 1. With MJ on the team, Nike began to dominate the market, and shoe contracts have never been the same since. How did Nike come to dominate the market? Innovation.

If you've never heard the name Tinker Hatfield before, don't feel bad; most people haven't. Hatfield is a former University of Oregon track athlete who competed under legendary coach Bill Bowerman. This college athlete-turned-architect-turned-shoe designer is considered one of the most famous sneaker icons in the world with a career spanning decades and such iconic designs as the Air Max and Michael Jordan collaborations. In fact, *Slam Magazine* once called him "the most important sneaker designer ever." Hatfield is responsible for the majority of Michael Jordan's shoe designs, from the Jordan IIIs (back when MJ was considering leaving Nike) to the Jordan IXs.

The once-proud Puma developed an appreciation for this kind of innovation. After a twenty-year absence from the hoops sneaker space, in 2018 the German company returned to action. Well aware that Nike and (to a lesser extent) Adidas had dominated the marketplace for a long time, Puma's executives understood that the only way to compete with the traditional shoe powers was by doing things differently.

So, the company re-entered performance basketball with a dynamic splash during that year's NBA draft, shocking the sneaker world by signing five of the top sixteen pro picks. It also announced a partnership with famed rapper Jay-Z, who became a creative consultant. The year after the signings, Adam Petrick, global director of brand and marketing told one publication, "I couldn't ask for a better partner in building the vision for what we're doing . . . Jay-Z is a savvy business partner who understands how the market works . . . He's also extraordinarily knowledgeable about the culture surrounding the game."[28]

The shoemaker's star-studded signings in 2018 included the top two picks: Deandre Ayton (Phoenix Suns) and Marvin Bagley III (Sacramento). Bagley's five-year footwear and endorsement deal generated the biggest waves since it was estimated to be the largest shoe deal since Kevin Durant's 2014 signing with Nike, which was valued between $265 million and $285 million. It was Puma's first NBA shoe deal since Vince Carter had signed in 1998, only to depart a year later for Nike. Bagley had been expected to sign with Nike too, since the swoosh-makers sponsored his AAU team in high school, and he was a national player of the year as a member of the Nike-sponsored Duke Blue Devils. Former sports marketing executive Sonny Vaccaro, who helped sign Jordan for Nike, told *The* (Portland) *Oregonian*, "This will send shock waves through the industry."[29]

The company also signed Kevin Knox (#9, New York Knicks), Michael Porter Jr., (#14, Denver), and Zhaire Smith (#16, also selected by Phoenix, but immediately traded to Philadelphia). Two years after the hubbub generated by Bagley's signing, Puma picked up the most recognizable—and unconventional—name in the 2020 NBA draft: LaMelo Ball. The son of LeVar Ball, LaMelo had a role in his family's Facebook Watch reality show (*Ball in the Family*), a signature shoe produced by his father's Big Baller Brand, and experience playing in Australia in 2019, when he won the National Basketball League's "Rookie of the Year" title.

"PUMA Basketball is still a relatively new space for us as far as our business goes," Curtis Begg, senior director of marketing at Puma Canada, told a publication there. "We've got a strong history of soccer in Europe, so for us to get into a North American team sport was critical. This is the kickoff to our third season in basketball, if you can believe it. And LaMelo has been a great addition; he's young and energetic and definitely marches to his own beat."[30]

A STORIED HISTORY

Puma's history with roundball stretches back nearly fifty years to 1973. That's when Walt "Clyde" Frazier became the first player in NBA history to get his own signature shoe. Others would follow, most notably Isaiah Thomas—one of my childhood idols—who wore Pumas in the 1990 NBA finals when his Detroit Pistons defeated the Portland Trail Blazers to claim back-to-back championships. Yet, it was a telling sign of the company's fading fortunes when their partnership with Thomas only lasted one season. Their run at other top players peaked with their 1998 deal with Carter.

The company spent the next two decades largely on the sidelines. With Nike dominating the basketball category with Air

Jordans, Kobe Bryant's signature line, and LeBron James's Air Zoom line, the competition wasn't even close. Adidas would rank a distant second with everything else up for grabs. But then Puma realized the trendsetters in the United States were basketball players. Of the "Big Four" (basketball, football, baseball, hockey), it was NBA players who were the larger-than-life figures influencing culture.

The big question was this: How was Puma going to disrupt the basketball shoe industry against the big boys? Their plan of attack came from capitalizing on persuading young people to choose them as alternative to the establishment represented by Nike and Adidas. Puma targeted the teen market, billing its sneakers as the "game changer," as their chief marketing executive, Curtis Begg, called it.

A report on the turnaround includes these interesting observations from Begg (and the publication):

"The time was right for us to come back, and I think a lot of it has to do with the opportunity off the court just as much as it does on the court . . . We're interested in the tunnel walk and making sure there's high visibility in moments like that, too. It's about the culture of basketball.'

"But the real question is: How can the brand contend with the kick titans that have commanded the space for so long? PUMA's attack plan is to offer kids an alternative to the establishment. Targeting younger consumers in the 14-to-18-year-old range, according to Begg, the

brand is positioning itself as a subversion of the sneaker
status quo—a cooler, out-of-the-box option."[31]

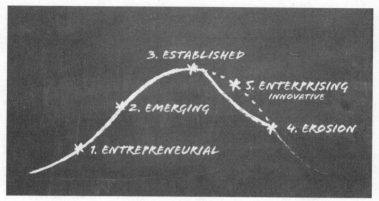

So, after an extended time of *erosion* in the shoe industry,
Puma was able to become innovative and turn its basketball
brand around. Whenever a company is in the *erosion* phase—and
in Puma's case, it was for two decades—they must, in order to
save the franchise/business/ organization/church from becoming
irrelevant or to emerge from irrelevance, enter the phase of *enterprising* (see graphic). Ideally, in the *emerging* phase, this is when
ideations and innovation would be applied and championed
by the lead visionary. That's in a perfect world. But if things
are moving too fast, and systems and structures have not been
implemented, then bad habits and practices can seep into the
organization. If complacency starts happening at the *established*
phase, an alarm must be sounded before a massive restructuring
or reorganization is needed to keep the company from going on

the operating table or being placed on life support. Whenever the disruption has to happen, it will always hurt. It's ideal to do it in the *emerging* phase and necessary in the *established* phase, but it's critical during *erosion*.

Historically, the building of the First Temple in Jerusalem is considered to be Solomon's greatest achievement.[32]

If *erosion* is taking place, that's when *enterprising* steps must also occur. Conditions may still erode while such *enterprise* is occurring, but leaders must act. This is where significant innovation, ideations, discipline, and tough decisions must be made in order to avoid bankruptcy, or even closing the doors for good.

CREATING A TURNAROUND

When Lisa and I assumed the leadership of our congregation, now called Inspire Church, we accepted the position as senior pastors of a place that had seen (repeatedly) difficult times and little growth over a span of thirteen years. Plus, people had experienced transitions in senior leadership on five different occasions. When we stepped in, a good weekend would have been one worship service attended by around sixty people. With only a few thousand dollars in the bank, we had no building and no office, and we met in a rented elementary school cafeteria for four hours on Sunday. The crazy thing was that we saw potential in the people and the opportunity.

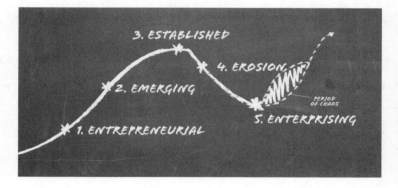

The church wasn't in an *erosion* phase anymore; it had already eroded. We didn't *enterprise* it. We had to start from scratch. We had to have the mindset of becoming *entrepreneurial* all over again. We needed to share a compelling enough vision of the future to change the mindset of the people. Those who opted to give it another shot with a sixth change in leadership needed to adopt this vision. For some, it wasn't fun because I had unknowingly introduced *chaos* into their lives. Dr. Sam Chand refers to chaos as the period when "the leaders'

urgency, hope, and bigger calling are combined with their followers' confusion, lethargy, and doubt."[33]

To gain some quick momentum to turn things around, we went "old school." An enthusiastic team of volunteers and I went door-to-door, placing door hangers/flyers on the front doorknobs of homes proclaiming a "new church" in town with a new name (chaos to most of the old faithful). We advertised on the radio, often worked remotely, and met periodically for coffee at Borders (a business that never transitioned and fell victim to Amazon, at a time when Amazon sold primarily books). We had two Sony Vaio laptops and two Nextel combo walkie-talkie/cell phones. (I mentioned these earlier and our denigrating reference to them as "next-to-hell" phones because they weren't any good.) For our office, we borrowed a loft at the top of a friend's custom cabinet warehouse.

As an aside when it comes to *erosion*, notice the names of Borders, Nextel, and Sony Vaio.

In 1972, Borders opened its first bookstore in Ann Arbor, Michigan, when brothers Tom and Louis Borders launched what would become one of the most notable book chains in the nation. Thirty-nine years later, there were more than five hundred superstores in the U.S. plus 175 in its Waldenbooks specialty segment, familiar to everyone who sailed through airports en route to their next flight. But year forty marked the beginning of the end: In February 2011, Borders filed for Chapter 11 bankruptcy protection and began liquidating assets of nearly half its stores. Too little too late; in July it began selling off everything else. Meanwhile Nextel merged with Sprint in 2005 to become Sprint/Nextel, with the Nextel network officially shutting down on June 30, 2013. And, while Sony is doing quite well in electronics, it no longer is in the computer business, having sold off its popular Vaio line in 2014.

A NEW PHASE

The *entrepreneurial* phase at Inspire lasted between two and three years; as things change, it's hard to define them by exact dates or time frames. We successfully recreated a healthy culture, and as I began to personally grow as a pastor and leader, we grew incrementally at a healthy pace. While I grew impatient with the way that we scaled, another church about five minutes away from our rented space exploded out of the gates and reached six hundred in attendance within the first year. After moving into a new building that accommodated their skyrocketing growth, they grew to more than three thousand by year three!

While I was happy for them, to be honest it took a lot for me to celebrate and be happy about our modest accomplishments. It took almost a decade to hit a thousand in average attendance. Yet, considering we started with about sixty people, our annual growth averaged 32.5 percent for each of those ten years. How many businesses do you know that grow at that rate? Likely not too many. That's even taking into consideration the people who left because of the chaos, moved on because of new military assignments, or transitioned away for a multitude of other reasons.

In addition, after year ten of this close to twenty-year journey, we started growing at a much faster rate. When we acquired a great space in a shopping center, it changed the trajectory of our future. In fact, I chronicled much of this story in my first book, titled *The Pound for Pound Principle* (which released in a new tenth-anniversary edition in the summer of 2020). A few years later I wrote a book entitled *Plateaus: Moving From Where You Are To Where You Want to Be*. In it, I talked about the different plateaus we encounter on our own personal journeys. From the point of view of an *emerging* organization that is on—or headed for—the peak of the *emerging* phase, it can quickly turn into a plateau if we do not implement change for the sake of continuing the mission.

King Solomon was the last leader of a united Israel.[34]

In the *emerging* phase of Inspire, I kept telling our leaders, "We aren't *there* yet." We still haven't been *there*, but that's where we are headed. I didn't want us to get comfortable and get stuck on a plateau, and eventually experience *erosion* and ultimately become irrelevant. When we reached the *established* phase, I was quite concerned about hitting a plateau, so we sought out an opportunity to create momentum. We looked at different buildings and sought large enough parcels of land to build a bigger home for our growing congregation. While our shopping center space was wonderful, we only leased the property.

THREE KEY PRINCIPLES

If I had known then what I know now, I would have loved to have understood the five phases that every organization goes through. But I was learning on the fly and doing the best I could. I wasn't able to wordsmith and articulate all the phases we went through, but I'm glad that I can now. Allow me to share three principles for turning things around.

1) *PINPOINT* WHERE YOU ARE

However, don't just pinpoint where things are at the moment; identify your organization's location on your own Sigmoid/Bell curve. Don't stop there; do the same thing with your personal life. There may be a correlation between both. It might call for some humility to be able to do something like this, but it's the first step to moving on to a better phase. Perhaps this is a place where you invite coaches and consultants into your life for counseling, advice, and suggestions. Solomon did not have wise counselors around him, but we can often learn from other people's mistakes. *That's* called wisdom. You don't have to experience everything for yourself to know if that's the route that you want to take (or not). Sometimes experience is overrated. You don't have to experience the same things, and you don't have to make the same mistakes that someone else has made.

2) IMPLEMENT BETTER *PRACTICES*

It's one thing to identify the situation: "Houston, we have a problem." It's an entirely different thing to know what to do, when to do it, and how to do it. This is where a lot of people get stuck. They get "analysis paralysis." This happens as leaders overanalyze data, sit on it for too long, and continually err on the side of caution to a fault. Then . . . nothing happens, or a window of opportunity closes.

In addition, if your best practices are outdated, start adopting better practices from places you have visited that inspire you because every best practice eventually becomes an outdated one. Several years ago, I had the privilege of traveling from Hawai'i to Johannesburg, South Africa, to visit the amazing Rivers Church, led by Andre and Wilma Olivier. I've been to a lot of churches, in some of the most beautiful buildings, led by some of the greatest people. But when it comes to the architecture, excellence in building design and function, and incredible hospitality, at Rivers I honestly felt what it must have been like for the Queen of Sheba when she saw Jerusalem for the first time. At times, I was speechless. I witnessed an experience on a whole different level. It inspired me to do some creative contextualization. Not to copycat, but to adapt certain aspects I observed into our own culture. It has forever altered my outlook. Indeed, it's one of the reasons I wrote this book.

3) TURN YOUR *PLATEAUS* (AND EROSION) INTO A LAUNCHING *PAD*

If you have ever witnessed a hang glider, you'll always see they're standing at the edge of a cliff and waiting for an updraft to carry them off the ground. Don't imitate a glider! One of the most crucial and seemingly hardest parts of the five organizational phases outlined by Dr. Sam Chand in Chapter Seven, is *enterprising*. How do you reinvent the wheel? How do you take what's been successful and adapt it to something new and fresh? How do you swing the pendulum of innovation and strategy? The truth is you will not find this to be an easy feat. However, I think we can all take a page out of The Walt Disney Company's playbook.

Let's look at Bob Iger who was CEO of The Walt Disney Company until early 2020 and now serves as executive chairman. When Iger stepped into his position in the fall of 2005, he inherited a company with a lack of success at the box office, disgruntled employees, and discontent in the Disney community as the company built on Mickey Mouse stepped away from animation. Hungry to bring innovation back to Disney, Iger had no choice but to pioneer.

So, what did he do? Well, for starters, he struck a deal with Apple genius Steve Jobs to buy Pixar Animation Studios—on the verge of its existing contract to distribute Pixar films coming to an end. Later, Iger acquired Marvel Entertainment and the

"Star Wars" and "Indiana Jones" franchises, one of his most controversial, and yet beneficial, decisions. In addition, toward the end of his tenure in the executive office, he bought 21st Century Fox and capitalized on these newly acquired franchises by monetizing them into action figures, toys, movies, and even theme parks.[35] Before stepping down, he also launched Disney Plus, a subscription, video-on-demand streaming service, which in its first sixteen months surpassed one hundred million subscribers globally (at a time when cable TV and satellite services had been hemorrhaging customers).

How did this turn out? Of the twenty top box office hits of all time, Disney had produced eleven of them under Iger's leadership. Disney's market value had grown from $48 billion to more than $257 billion. Outlining the steps Iger took to reinvent Disney, British business executive and author Peter Fisk wrote: "Disney stands out as one of the few corporations to have managed to transform themselves, not just to survive but to thrive, in today's world of digital disruption and incredible change. Usually we turn to start-ups to learn how to embrace digital platforms and the new zeitgeist, but Disney is a shining example of how large and established organizations can do it too."[36]

So, what does this all mean? *Enterprise* takes vision to see what no one else sees. Bob Iger illustrates how this can be done. However, innovation doesn't come without its fair share of criticism. When Iger bought Marvel Entertainment for $4 billion, he met an overwhelming amount of skepticism because not many saw what he did. And yet, look at the amount of success this franchise has brought. Anyone heard of "The Avengers" series? A $4 billion deal had grossed more than $22 billion by early 2021. Not too shabby.

UP THE CHARTS

Puma turned things around after twenty years in basketball shoe purgatory. Disney did it when it was losing a generation's interest. No matter where you can pinpoint your location on the curve, it's never too late to turn it back *up the chart and to the right*.

At the end of the day, in the face of *erosion*, you must enter into the *enterprise* phase. Reinventing the wheel doesn't mean you have to start from scratch, but it does mean you need finesse to know where to prune, where to adjust, and how to move forward. It's not about working harder; it's about working smarter.

I always tell my staff, "Blessed are the flexible, for they will never be bent out of shape." I like to think of *enterprising* exactly like that. Remain flexible to the strategy so you can seize all potential opportunities to turn your business around for the better. Let me make this clear. The *enterprise* phase is not just helpful—it's critical. It is the only way to keep you and your business from plateauing in your quest to provide excellent service to your customers—and thrive in the future.

READ THIS BEFORE YOU MOVE FORWARD:

As you start to pinpoint where you are, work toward implementing better practices and turn your plateaus into a launching pad, I want to offer you a word of encouragement. It's not over for you. Maybe you feel a bit discouraged thinking of the work that's ahead of you, or maybe you feel like it's over, but it's not. Even though we're moving into the final chapter of *That Doesn't Just Happen*, the final chapter of your life has not been written yet. There are still new opportunities, fresh insights, and key relationships to come. My prayer and my hope for you is you will learn to see things differently because, at some level, failure can always make you better. Failure is a cruel teacher, but lessons learned can be a catalyst for improvement. I believe in you, and you can do this.

If you've learned lessons, they may be ones you would not have learned otherwise in success. Why? Because failure is a cruel teacher and frustration can be a catalyst for improvement.

KEEP ENTERPRISING IF YOU WANT TO KEEP RISING

Today more than ever, building an enterprising organization that will last as it offers the best is not just about being resilient. It's also about being flexible!

10

W*hen I was looking for examples of great companies—those worldwide brands that kept moving up the charts and seemed to always innovate and kept people uttering the three Ws ("Wait. What? Wow!")—two immediately came to mind: Netflix and Tesla. These two companies are prime examples of being enterprising before they experience erosion. From the outset, in the entrepreneurial phase and into the emerging phase, they seemed to leapfrog over obstacles through innovation and ideation, almost avoiding erosion like the plague.*

Enter Netflix. I briefly mentioned it when I discussed Blockbuster Video (Chapter Seven). This once-familiar chain figuratively and literally became extinct because of its inability to innovate fast enough. Hung up on late fees, Blockbuster didn't just plateau; it died fighting on the hill of profitable late charges without considering the resentment it created among millions of customers. When Netflix founder and CEO Reed Hastings launched Netflix, he set out to build a world-class office culture that was better than at his previous company, a debugging computer programmer named Purify Software. Building on that culture failure, he took those lessons into his new company. But he didn't start and end with culture. (Yes, we can all agree with the adage that culture eats strategy for breakfast.) You have to have a great strategy to complement a great culture, and vice versa. Then you might have your cake and eat it, too.

THE THREE Ws

Hastings did the three Ws when Netflix started sending DVDs in the mail (remember that?) without any late fees before evolving into a largely streaming video service. In 2013 it also branched into film and television production, regularly winning Emmy Awards, Oscars, and Golden Globes (collectively more than 100 to date). Early on, Hastings could see he needed a team that could develop a first-class logistics operation for shipping DVDs. And at some point, that same team would have to forget all its logistical experience and pivot to online streaming—from scratch. That was one . . . massive . . . gigantic leap.

But wait, there's more! Even when fewer than one in ten households had broadband internet in the 1990s, Hastings anticipated future market demand for online streaming of movies, television series (seasons), and documentary series, investing $750 million into the business from the sale of his previous venture. Instead of refining the DVD business for another decade, which would have ultimately crashed, Netflix kept looking beyond its view of the summit to summits and peaks beyond.

Next, they were first in line to have the Netflix app installed in every smart TV that was sold. They knew their customer and accordingly upgraded their technological ability. Finally, Netflix started producing original content, becoming the ultimate source for entertainment. In the early days of COVID-19 on February 3, 2020, Netflix stock was trading at $358 on the NASDAQ; on September 1 it hit its 2020 peak at more than

$556 per share (and by Inauguration Day in January 2021 had surpassed $582).

NETFLIX LESSONS AS YOU ENTERPRISE

1) CULTURE IS CRITICAL.

I know I wrote a lot about this in Parts 1 and 2, but Netflix took this to another level. There's a reason why Netflix was able to outmaneuver a company like Blockbuster when the latter was one hundred times its size. But "it's not a story of competition . . . but of cooperation, a cultural flourishing that took place within Netflix's headquarters."[37] (For more on culture, refer to Chapter 4.)

2) INNOVATION ISN'T ONE-TIME-ONLY.

You must constantly reinvent yourself. As I write these words, there are thousands of businesses and churches that are struggling; many did not survive the COVID-19 lockdowns or the flare-ups that followed in late 2020. Whether because of an aversion to innovate, a lateness in making the changes, or an unwillingness to accept the new realities of the pandemic-influenced economy, they still have not made the necessary adjustments to thrive beyond survival.

Even at the church I pastor, we are still having to instill the idea in our staff that we can't put all our eggs in the basket of in-person gatherings in our buildings. We must embrace the facts of the "new reality." Namely, that most of our people are watching and participating online. Many of the people online have been hesitant to come back, and some may never return. But we've also have reached new audiences—for lack of a better term—who are joining us from literally all over the globe. "Zoom Church" is no longer an idle phrase.

Before March 2020, Inspire's average online weekend attendance would have been somewhere between seven hundred and nine hundred viewers. Before the shutdowns hit Hawai'i, we were already anticipating what was eventually going to happen to the rest of the United States. I prepared myself as I watched friends in countries like Singapore and other parts of Asia, trying to gauge how they were reacting to and responding to what hit their region (since the outbreak originated in the Far East). So, for two weeks we were ready to "flip the switch" when the government gave word that we could not meet.

As a result, in the early weeks of the pandemic, we went from seven hundred online viewers to sixty thousand per weekend—I'm talking as measured by unique visits on Facebook, YouTube, Church Online, Instagram, Twitch, Periscope, Twitter, and Tik Tok. We have experienced a drop-off since then, but today we are much clearer on whom we are reaching. Additionally, we are also preparing for the day (if and when) that we may not be able to place our online content on some of these platforms.

The online environment spanned more than church services. We also conducted six regional online summits in the US, South Africa, New Zealand, Australia, Asia, and South

America—something we wouldn't have dared to attempt before 2020. There were many different ways we had attempted to reach people and make a global impact for the Lord; there are almost too many to mention. But we wouldn't have been able to do all of this if it were not for the healthy culture of a staff who was willing to do whatever it took. And, we had the technology to pull it off. We also hired extra staff in the creative media, web, and technology departments. We changed staff roles more times in a year than in the previous three. Plus, the geeks here have become the "rock stars," and I love it! We keep *enterprising* so we can keep rising!

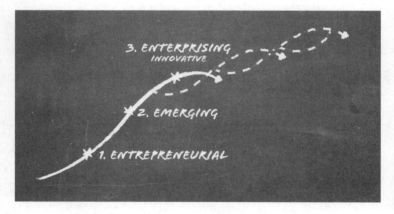

As we emerged, *enterprising* wasn't the only thing we implemented during the worldwide shutdown. We were already doing our best to innovate and adapt as we felt God lead us. We've heard the old saying that "art imitates life," but I think the world imitates the church—churches that are excellent in what they do, that is.

A few years ago, I had to lead our church through a rebranding of our name. It wasn't an easy thing to do when there were loyalties involved, mixed with my self-imposed expectations. I resisted the idea of changing our name from Hope Chapel West Oʻahu. (Try to say that ten times fast!) The Hope name formed my church roots, was tied to island history, and gave us a corporate identity. However, because there were so many churches that included *Hope* in their name, it also made it difficult for people to find us. Even on Google, we never appeared until page two, and nobody I know goes that far on a Google search.

But I didn't do it for these reasons: 1) we needed a kick start, 2) it was fashionable to rebrand, 3) something bad had happened, and we needed to distance ourselves, or 4) we weren't growing, so we needed a new name. Those are some of the typical reasons for a rebranding. Instead, we took this step because I had a dream one night that we changed our name. And when you get dreams like that, they're not ordinary dreams of the variety that stem from consuming too much pizza the night before. This was a heaven-inspired dream.

Despite this awesome experience, it took almost two years before I implemented the change, and we switched to Inspire Church. We needed to hold lots of meetings on a variety of levels in order to get buy-in from our leadership. I also needed denominational approval and the approval of my former senior pastor. Since Pastor Ralph was the founder of the Hope Chapel movement of churches, and I was one of his spiritual sons, I found it a serious and somewhat daunting task to pitch the idea to him. I didn't want it to be received as being disloyal. But when I met with him, it was exactly the opposite! He enthusiastically gave us his blessing! Rebranding wasn't easy by any stretch of the imagination, and it wasn't cheap! But I'm so glad that we did it. Rather than distancing us, it differentiated and distinguished us. Plus, it made it much easier for those outside the church to find us on the internet!

TESLA: AMAZING INNOVATOR

Tesla Motor Company is one of the most amazing and compelling success stories of the twenty-first century. Founder and CEO Elon Musk wasn't content to dominate the burgeoning electric car industry. Considered a flat-out genius, he was the cofounder of PayPal, the electronic payment system that was sold to eBay in 2002 for $1.5 billion, and is the founder of Space Exploration Technologies (Space X), which has plans to put people on Mars.

Musk had a tiered or *phase* approach to scale his car business by doing the following in phase one: "Create a low volume car which would be expensive." (That makes sense because the lower the production levels, the higher the costs.) "Use that money to develop a medium volume car at a lower price . . . Use that money to create an affordable, high volume car . . . and . . . provide solar power."[38] Musk used the money he netted from the sale of PayPal to start the first phase, and the rest is history.

King Solomon reigned for about forty years.[39]

However, he also phased the company and scaled it, step by step, to where it is today. Creating a low volume car meant something smaller and simpler, but most things would be done by hand. Next, he would expand different models of Teslas to be able to offer the consumer options like a sedan, a compact SUV, and—coming soon to a Tesla showroom near you—a pickup truck. Plus, to provide sustainability and literally empower Tesla owners' homes to become their own power plants, the company plans to provide solar panels and batteries. In other words, Musk is developing an ecosystem of products that are dependent on one another while being independent of fossil fuels and, of course, sustainable.

TESLA LESSONS AS YOU ENTERPRISE

Many of the following six lessons originated with a consultation I had about seven years ago with Dr. Sam Chand, although the points on sensibility and flexibility are mine. The primary things we can glean from Tesla's success include the following:

1) Scalability: Asks the question, *"Can we grow this?"* When we scale our business structure for growth, we have to ask the hard questions like, "Do we expand staff to keep growing? Will the current team help us grow? Do we grow and then add to the team?"

Elon Musk used the principle of scalability to design Tesla's business model with far-sighted wisdom. The success of one product would be the seed investment for the next line of products, and so on. He didn't immediately come out with mass production of his electric vehicles; he started small and built upon the success of each phase. Brilliant! In other words, he did not overreach and place the company in jeopardy from the start. He scaled his business model for growth. Solomon, on the other hand, overextended the nation of Israel with building projects. Therefore, he needed to overtax the people in order to continue paying the construction costs. It might have been scalable in the beginning, but it wouldn't prove to be sustainable.

2) Replicability: Asks the question, *"Can we duplicate this?"* Also, *"Is this franchise-able?"*

Is this model duplicatable in other contexts, or does it become its own, unique, stand-alone model? For Tesla, the replicability question was answered by the Tesla factory pumping out models X, Y, 3, S, and (coming soon) the Tesla Cybertruck, with an estimated five hundred thousand trucks pre-ordered by early 2021.

One of the big questions I have regarding Solomon and the Queen of Sheba is whether she replicated anything she might have seen on her trip to Jerusalem. Was there a shift in excellence and protocols, in architectural design? Was what she saw duplicatable? It is if you can creatively adapt what you see somewhere else.

When I gave up my job at American Airlines to become a full-time youth pastor in my early years of ministry, I never thought I would fly again to different destinations. I resigned myself to the fact that on a youth pastor's salary I couldn't afford to travel, and I would be home in Hawai'i for most of my time. But God has a way of always giving back to you more than what you sacrificed. Now, my passport has been stamped with so many different country seals, I've even had to add more pages to it. I've been to more destinations than I could have ever ask for or imagined! And most of the time, it's because I've been invited to do what I do: preach at great churches and coach some of the most amazing people on the planet!

Everywhere I've gone to visit as a guest speaker I've asked myself if I could replicate what I see. We started our Inspire Collective because of the inspiration I received from other models. We replicated other versions to our context and creatively adapted and ideated them to fit what we do and who we are. Then Dr. Sam Chand and Martijn van Tilborgh and our Collective teams scaled my local model to become a global brand that launched in the spring of 2021!

I've seen excellence in so many other churches that I've had the privilege of visiting. I must say the perception people once had of the church doing things at a "good enough" level is something I don't see often, although I know it happens. Excellence means doing the best you can with what you have and is not necessarily about how big your budget is; a bigger budget helps but not always.

3) Marketability: Asks the question, *"Can we communicate this?"* On one hand, the question is posed because internal communication requires excellence. When team members are brought into the loop of decisions that can affect the overall good of the organization, they feel valued. Excellent communication contributes to the healthy culture you are building. On the other hand, marketability helps move the needle with what you are promoting.

The marketability of a startup car company originating with a single, billionaire businessmen may sound exciting. But with each phase of Musk's master plan (written in 2006) came great scrutiny, criticism, and even ridicule. However, each completed phase brought success, which bred momentum on his brand, which increased Tesla's marketability without Musk spending a dollar on TV advertising. It was primarily word-of-mouth, helped along by some social media plugs, but the owners actually became the sales force. The release of the early Tesla models turned heads, and proud owners were happy to sing the praises of their sensible investments.

As I mentioned previously, kings and dignitaries came to sit and learn from Solomon and glean his wisdom. Today they would be called raving fans. They came by word-of-mouth and were hosted by Solomon and his staff. What Solomon had built was marketable, and it was communicated.

4) Sensibility: Asks the question, *"Does it make sense?"* The Tesla business plan, products, and the ecosystem all make

sense—a whole lot of it! Do your plans to scale your organization make sense for the season, the context, and the market where you are located? Or, does it make more sense to wait?

A few years ago, Inspire Church purchased three acres of land to build a new multipurpose facility. Our goal is for it to have five streams of income. We have designed a building that will have two basketball/volleyball courts and a weight training facility dedicated to speed, quickness, and jumping. Next, we have a dedicated space for a performing arts and dance studio, audio and visual recording studios, and office space available for lease on the second floor, where various medical professionals can set up their practices. We also will offer a café operation selling the best coffee, cappuccinos, and cold-pressed juices, and a variety of salads and healthy sandwich options. And of course, a state-of-the-art auditorium for conferences and church services on the weekend.

Essentially, we have designed a "Wellness Center" for the body, mind, soul, and spirit. When parents drop off their children at the dance studio for lessons or at the gym for training, they will not have to leave our facility. They will socialize, get work done, or participate in a connect group in our coffee lobby. We are attempting to create our own ecosystem where it just makes sense. Additionally, we are pouring a concrete pad that is thick enough to be able to house a logistics facility, should we decide in the future that we want to sell the building in order to have other options. That *just makes sense.*

5) Sustainability: Asks the question, "*Will this last?*" I'm sure Tesla Motor Company is here to stay. Although it is not the first to build electric vehicles, it isn't going anywhere anytime soon.

"Will this last?" is a great question we should keep asking ourselves. Earlier I mentioned *Bigger, Faster Leadership* by Dr. Sam Chand. If you haven't gotten that book yet, make sure you get it—after you're done recommending this book to ten other people! In Dr. Chand's book, he asks the sustainability question and addresses our systems and our structures. Do you have those in place so that, whatever you plan on building, it can be sustained? Solomon, his kingdom, and his lifestyle were not sustainable. Now if Solomon had followed God's instructions for his personal life, then the kingdom that he built could have been sustained. However, at the rate he was going, there was no way that was possible. Sadly, it eventually split in half, and the former glory of a unified Israel did not happen again. Though I believe it will someday, and it will be better than ever!

We all want to build something that will outlast us. We want to leave a legacy. This is true for almost everyone, because nobody wants to see what they have poured their heart and soul and resources into fall apart in the end. This also applies to our personal lives. Can we sustain the pace that we are working at today? Can we sustain the payments for the lifestyle where we live? We can think of so many other questions about sustainability, but this is where sensibility complements sustainability. I know you probably have faith for more, and that you are believing that the best is yet to come. But let's approach what we build with sensibility and sustainability for a more permanent and lasting legacy.

6) Flexibility: Asks the question, *"Can we shift when needed?"*

There are two phrases we have ingrained into our culture at Inspire:

» We are built to change.

Jim Collins, whom I mentioned earlier, wrote another incredible book called *Built to Last*. After reading it years ago, I decided to adjust the phrase. Instead of "built to last," we would be "built to change" so that we would last. Blockbuster, the previously mentioned video store chain that collapsed a decade ago, wasn't ready to make the changes necessary, so it held on until the bitter end with a business model that proved to be its undoing. In order to be built to change, we created a culture of flexibility among our staff. We decided that some people would have to be Swiss army knives, and some people had to be Ginsus.

King Solomon died of natural causes in 931 B.C. at the age of eighty. His son, Rehoboam, took the throne which eventually led to the erosion of the Kingdom of Israel.[40]

We all know what a Swiss army knife is; I'd be willing to bet that some of you have one in a kitchen pantry or a bathroom vanity drawer. Mine is in the top drawer to the left, just under my countertop. The great thing about a Swiss army knife is its multiple functions. It doesn't just cut things. Some offer more than two dozen uses, such as acting as a screwdriver, a can opener, fish scaler, pliers, micro scissors, and even a toothpick! And of course, you can slice an apple with it or whittle a stick.

However, a Ginsu is a specialty knife. It pretty much serves one purpose. The ubiquitous nature of these direct-marketed knives goes back decades, when infomercials in the late 1970s and early '80s fueled sales of more than two million sets and made Ginsu's name nearly as familiar to late-night viewers as Ronco (and Ginsu outlasted Ronco, which collapsed in 2018). A Ginsu knife will cut all day long with one basic function. You can't use it as a screwdriver or as a toothpick, but it will cut for you.

On our staff, we have a few people who are more like Ginsu knives, such as accountants and attorneys, who are valuable to our team. Just as valuable are people of the Swiss army knife variety. Their flexibility enables them to do more; they are multipurpose and have different skill sets, which have been developed through a culture of flexibility. That way, the whole organization is *built to change* so that we are *built to last*. We are able to pivot, change directions, and flip the switch when necessary.

When the lockdowns of 2020 arrived, just a few days before the government flipped the switch, we were able to shift from eighty percent in-person attendance and twenty percent online to zero percent in person and one hundred percent online. In our healthy and thriving culture, our team is able to understand that the needs of the organization rank above personal preferences. So our ability to build to change doesn't just help us last, it helps us build *better*.

» We are built to be flexible.

Being built to change so you can be built to last so you can be built better comes because of flexibility. That's why, for more than a decade, I've embraced the saying I mentioned previously: *Blessed are the flexible, for they will never be bent out of shape.* A team that is flexible is critical to *enterprising* for the future. It doesn't mean we lack strategy or take advantage of our people, knowing they will forgive a multitude of poor planning decisions. No. Doing that would mean frustrating them because nobody wants to work for someone who lacks clear vision and maintains a haphazard strategy, overusing this phrase to become an excuse for poor leadership. However, it is true that when a team is flexible because that trait is built into the culture, they are more forgiving when adjustments need to be made.

To thrive in the twenty-first century, we must be flexible enough to shift directions and adjust as our world changes. New industries that have done so have thrived as a result. Who would have thought the plexiglass business would be positioned to be a sustainable success story? Beyond making 1990s style pulpits and podiums, and trophies and plaques for athletic events, the plexiglass business is a prime example of companies that have enterprised in today's world. During the pandemic, traditional rum manufacturers in Hawai'i added a line of disinfectants to their products. Netflix enterprised from distributing DVDs by mail to streaming video. Uber started with transporting people from one destination to another, and as it grew, added Uber Eats, a name now as familiar as the ridesharing portion of its business. Amazon, once considered "the largest bookstore in the world," enterprised to become the world's largest retailer of goods and services and has been giving Netflix a run for its money in the streaming video sector.

You've likely heard the old saying, *If you keep doing what you've been doing, then you'll always get what you've always got.* I know that's not good English, but I like how it transmits the idea. Today more than ever, building an *enterprising* organization that will last as it offers the best is *not just about being resilient. It's also about being flexible!*

At the end of the day, it doesn't matter what you build if what you build is not sustainable. And in order to build something sustainable, you have to begin innovating. Take the time now to *enterprise,* so you can ultimately finish better.

CONCLUSION

If you've made it this far in *That Doesn't Just Happen*, I'm positive you're feeling inspired and ready to take your organization (or even your life) to another level of excellence. I want to encourage you to take excellence with you wherever you go. In the marketplace. In the staff lounge. In your home. In your board meetings. In your daily life. Excellence will distinguish you from the ordinary.

I'm rooting for you to create and curate an environment where you can flourish, to creatively adapt principles from this book into your own corporate or cultural context and to reinvent yourself or your company in a way that will help you build to last, build to change, and finish better. No matter what you do, apply these principles to any area of your life, and you will accelerate your excellence to a whole new level!

There is one last, major takeaway I want to give to you. Beyond the principles, the journey, and the stories and observations, there is something much more precious than the gold King Solomon adorned his kingdom with, and much more costly than the silver and spices the Queen of Sheba offered as gifts. (Yes, spices were and are still important.) Towards the end of Solomon's life, he lamented, "But as I looked at everything I had worked so hard to accomplish, it was all so meaningless—like chasing the wind. There was nothing really worthwhile anywhere" (Ecclesiastes 1:11, NIV).

Let those words sink in: *meaningless; like chasing the wind.* Why? Because he became his own king in his eyes and never truly humbled himself before the Lord. Solomon forgot who his

Source was—the Source allowing him to reign as king, and the Fountain from Whom all good things flow. Solomon eventually lived like he was a self-made man and not God-made, but it doesn't have to be that way for us. There is One who is behind Solomon's excellence. One whose wisdom is beyond comprehension. His name is Jesus, and He can add so much more to this life. In fact, He is the spice of life!

You see, although King Solomon and the Queen of Sheba exchanged lavish amounts of gifts and bestowed honor on one another, Jesus has done that and more. In fact, God is the Founder of excellence, and the greatest gift ever given to humankind is His son, Jesus. It's as John 3:16 says: "For God so loved the world that he gave his one and only Son, that whoever believes in him shall not perish but have eternal life" (NIV). And not only that, but God has lavished us with His gift of love. First John 3:1 says, "See how very much our Father loves us, for he calls us his children, and that is what we are!" (NIV)

If you're really wanting to expand upon your excellence, take a page out of God's playbook. After all, where do you think Solomon got all that wisdom?

Let's Do This!

—*Mike Kai*

APPENDIX

HISTORICAL PERSPECTIVE

For those interested in additional historical perspective, the following may help you understand more about my search for more information about Solomon and the Queen of Sheba, who was so enraptured by the King of Israel. The more I read about them in the Bible and various historical records, the more intrigued I became. In the midst of the Bible chronicling the House of David and the transition of the kingdom of Israel splitting into two kingdoms (Judah to the south and retaining the name, Israel, to the north)—and eventually the diaspora to Assyria and Babylon—we have this jewel of an exchange that captures our imagination. It leaves us asking questions:

» Who was this queen? What was her name?

» What was she like, and who was her king?

» How could one afford to give away so much gold as a gift?

» Who was this beautiful woman of African descent? If she had any offspring, who were they and where are they now?

» What was it that took her breath away? How could someone with so much influence and wealth, and accustomed to excellence in her own context, be so awestruck?

To provide some perspective on what this king built calls for a quick history lesson, as related by 1 Kings 3:5–14. To start with, Solomon's father was David, the second king of Israel, and its greatest. David was especially notable since he followed insecure, mentally ill, and self-centered King Saul. Yet David would not become the king who built the majestic, bejeweled, internationally renowned temple for the great God, Yahweh, in the capital city of Jerusalem. It was in David's heart to build the temple, but God wouldn't allow that.

The reason stems from David's history as a man of war. Now, he was a giant-slayer and a fierce warrior who united the tribes of Israel and Judah. Yet, as David grew older, he realized that while he lived in a beautiful palace, the Ark of the Covenant was still being kept in a tent. This ark contained the sacred objects of Moses' time on earth. It contained a jar of manna (These coriander-like seed wafers fell from heaven every morning to feed the more than estimated two million Hebrews who crossed the Red Sea and into the wilderness. It was their breakfast for forty years!), Aaron's budded staff (a miracle), and the Ten Commandments. The lid contained two cherubim, face-to-face, and between them, God's presence dwelled. To house such sacred things in a tent? David saw this as a serious oversight. The God of Israel did not have a suitable and proper house in Jerusalem. While God wouldn't let David build it, He would set up Solomon to do so.

To prepare, David made all the necessary arrangements to build a temple suitable for Israel's glorious God, hiring highly skilled architects and assembling the best engineers. David reached out to his friend, King Hiram of Tyre, to supply the finest cedar and cypress wood, which was shipped from his kingdom down the Mediterranean coast to Israel. David enlisted the finest craftsmen: carpenters, stone carvers, goldsmiths, silversmiths, weavers, and bronze artisans. He secured silver to pay their wages. Nevertheless, God did not want David to build the temple because he had much blood on his hands from years of battle. Instead, God chose Solomon, a man of peace, to build it.

So, David made painstaking preparations to set up Solomon with everything he would need to build the glorious temple David had envisioned for Yahweh. He stockpiled gold, silver, and bronze; the finest carved limestone blocks, cedar, and cypress; ivory, fine linen, and tapestry; and other fine materials that Solomon would need to complete the work. David called on all his contacts to the north, east, and south, requesting the absolute best materials they had for his God. In other words, David did all he possibly could to set up his son for success with this monumental building project. Herein lie more principles:

1. MAKE EXCELLENT REQUESTS

Principle: If you could ask God for
anything, what would it be?

God had chosen Solomon to build the First Temple. To do this, Solomon would have to succeed his father on the throne of Israel. Technically, a king could designate his chosen successor to the throne. Traditionally, this role would go to the oldest living son, but influenced by his wife Bathsheba, David had Solomon (his tenth son) anointed as his successor.

For the sake of brevity, I am summarizing the passage from 1 Kings 3. Following David's death, Solomon sacrificed a lavish one thousand burnt offerings to God. Later that evening, God appeared to Solomon in a dream and asked, "What do you want? Ask, and I will give it to you!" Here I should pause to mention the fact that God appearing to Solomon in a dream is pretty notable stuff. It's amazing God would appear to any of us in a dream, right? God can still do that and still does. God chose to appear to Solomon on this occasion to encourage him as the new king of Israel and to affirm Solomon's profound devotion to Yahweh.

Equally notable are Solomon's responses in the interaction that follows. Solomon praised God for the faithfulness the Lord showed in keeping His promise to David—that one of his descendants would always sit on his throne. Then he continued with the comment that he was like a small child who didn't know his way around, so he needed God's help to govern. Two things impress me about this:

1) Solomon's demonstration of humility. He was the king at a time when that meant complete authority and control, yet he referred to himself as a little child when it came to shouldering his responsibilities.

2) His acknowledgment of God keeping His promises. This is quite significant, since one of the blessings of the original covenant God made with Abraham in Genesis 22:17

was that Abraham would have so many descendants he couldn't count them. So what, you say? Consider that more than a millennium passed between Abraham's death and the beginning of Solomon's reign. This shows that God always keeps His promises. While circumstances and ordinary human limitations may prevent you from *always* keeping your promises, when it comes to great customer service, honoring your word is certainly a worthwhile goal to keep in mind.

The obvious awe and respect Solomon had for this kind of God emerged in his next statement, where he asked for the understanding he would need to govern Israel. Wouldn't it be amazing if this were the prayer of everybody who was elected to office? Imagine how conditions might differ if leaders said, "God, I'm new at this, and these people are too numerous, so please give me a wise and understanding heart, that I might be the mayor of Honolulu . . . that I might be the governor of this state . . . that I might be the president of this great nation. Lord, let me have wisdom."

2. BUILD WITH WISDOM AND EXCELLENCE

Principle: If you're going to do
something, do it right.

The Lord was pleased that Solomon had asked for wisdom. In response, He told Solomon that because he had asked for wisdom to govern with justice instead of long life, wealth, or victory over his enemies, He would give him the kind of wise and understanding heart that no one heretofore had possessed, or would have afterward. Not only would Solomon be the greatest king, God would throw in riches and fame to boot. And, if Solomon followed His commands just as his father David had, God would grant him long life. Talk about answered prayer!

You need to know this background to appreciate why Solomon had greater wisdom than any other ruler on earth and became richer and wiser than any king who ever lived. This is why people from every nation, including the Queen of Sheba, came to consult him and learn about the wisdom God had given him. Solomon wrote and collected thousands of proverbs, many of which are preserved in the biblical Book of Proverbs. Ecclesiastes is based on Solomon's exploration of the meaning of life, and the Song of Solomon is an epic love story based on his life. He was so full of wisdom he would later write, "A house is built by wisdom and becomes strong through good sense. Through knowledge its rooms are filled with all sorts of precious riches and valuables" (Proverbs 24:3-4, NIV).

Indeed, by his God-given wisdom, Solomon built the "House of Yahweh," the official name of Solomon's Temple in Jerusalem. By wisdom, Solomon also built a magnificent palace in Jerusalem that was more glorious than David's palace. And by wisdom, Solomon built the walls of Jerusalem and rebuilt three powerful fortress cities to defend the main crossroads into the heartland of Israel. He also built a fleet of ships and an ocean-going port on the Red Sea. In addition, Solomon established towns as supply centers and others where he could station horses and chariots. He built everything he desired in Jerusalem, Lebanon, and throughout his entire realm.

I hope this provides you with a fuller picture of Solomon's managerial skill, foresight, and enormous reserves. In modern vernacular, he was *the man*!

The Old Testament says it took seven years for Solomon to build the temple and thirteen years to build his palace. Though both were magnificent, world-class buildings, they were completed in record time because of the preparations that had been made by King David ahead of King Solomon's rule, and because of the wisdom Solomon used in directing these projects. With the plans David had prepared for the temple, Solomon constructed everything to those exact specifications.

Ordinarily, building projects of this magnitude take decades, even more than a century, to complete. India's famed Taj Mahal took twenty-three years. King Herod's renovation of the second Jerusalem Temple and expansion of the Temple Mount complex took eighty-four years after he started work in 20 B.C. St. Basil's Cathedral in Moscow took 123 years. St. Peter's Basilica in Vatican City required 144 years. The building of Italy's Leaning Tower of Pisa lasted for 199. Construction of the Great Wall of China continued for two millennia.

THE WONDER OF EXCELLENCE

The First Temple was an impressive sight. It included a bronze platform that was 7 ½ feet long, 5 ½ feet wide, and 4 ½ feet high. (Instead of just reading about it, get out a tape measure and mark that off and you may get a more realistic picture.) After Solomon placed it in the outer courtyard, he stood on the platform, knelt in front of everyone, lifted his hands toward heaven, and prayed a lengthy prayer. This was no ordinary "thank you for the food" summation, but a heartfelt oration filled with praise and acknowledgment of God's supremacy and sovereignty, as well as reminders of His promises to David. He called on God to deliver justice, hear from heaven, and forgive the people of Israel if they disobeyed Him.

To give you an idea of the significance of this ceremony, when Solomon finished praying, fire flashed down from heaven and burned up the burnt offerings and sacrifices people had placed there. The glory of God filled the temple with such magnificence that even the priests couldn't enter. In response, the people fell facedown on the ground and worshiped and praised God. Then Solomon and the people followed up by offering a sacrifice of 22,000 cattle and 120,000 sheep and goats as the Levites blew trumpets and sang praises to the Lord. This all touched off a seven-day-long festival. And you thought Super Bowl parties were special!

Later, God appeared to Solomon to let him know how much the First Temple meant to Him and to the people who would call on Him for help. He told Solomon He had heard his prayer and had chosen this as the place for making sacrifices. In other words, this temple would hold a special status in the nation's worship of God, meaning it would also have a special place in the hearts and minds of the Israelites. Sometimes we discount the symbolic significance that churches, great halls, and monuments play in our consciousness, how we think about ourselves, and how we act as a result.

A CULTURE OF EXCELLENCE

After the completion and dedication of the temple of Yahweh, Solomon commenced building a new palace for his sizable family and numerous household servants. In fact, out of necessity the palace he built was much larger than the temple. Once completed, Solomon's palace—which he named the "Palace of the Forest of Lebanon"—contained more than 45,000 square feet, with a 3,375 square-foot grand hall, 45 side rooms, and an entry porch. Solomon spent nearly twice as long on his palace as the temple and even temporarily went into debt to King Hiram of Tyre in order to fund completion of the project.

In the process of designing and constructing all of his buildings and cities, Solomon was building something else: a culture of excellence throughout his kingdom. The Bible describes officials and rulers from near and far (including the Queen of Sheba) coming to gaze on his magnificent building projects and ask questions about Solomon's fabled wisdom. The queen's reaction symbolizes how people felt. First Kings 10:4-5 relates her feeling overwhelming and amazed at the food Solomon had served, the organization of his officials and their fine clothing, his cupbearers, and Solomon's burnt offerings in the temple. If you can wrap your mind around this, the Queen of Sheba gave Solomon a gift of nine thousand pounds of gold, plus great quantities of spices and precious jewels. Given the valuation of gold in late 2020, her gift of gold alone was worth more than $200 million (cue jaws dropping).

The temple that Solomon built was among the great wonders of the world at that time. It was completed in 957 B.C. and Solomon's palace in 944 B.C. Both remained in active use for more than 370 years.

ENDNOTES

1   William Cook, "Charles and Ray Eames: The couple who shaped the way we live," BBC/Culture, December 18, 2017, https://www.bbc.com/culture/article/20171218-charles-and-ray-eames-the-couple-who-shaped-the-way-we-live.

2   Cook, "Charles and Ray Eames: The couple who shaped the way we live"

3   "Charles and Ray Eames," Wikipedia, https://en.wikipedia.org/wiki/Charles_and_Ray_Eames.

4   Jake Strom, "Why Outsourcing Customer Service Kills Purpose-Driven Brands," Organizational Change, December 12, 2019, https://sustainablebrands.com/read/organizational-change/why-outsourcing-customer-service-kills-purpose-driven-brands.

5   Goodreads, "Excellence Wins Quotes," https://www.goodreads.com/work/quotes/67440898-excellence-wins-a-no-nonsense-guide-to-becoming-the-best-in-a-world-of.

6   Horst Schulze, "Hiring Decisions that Can Make or Break the Grandest Strategies," Leader to Leader, vol. 2019, issue 93, John Wiley online library, https://onlinelibrary.wiley.com/doi/abs/10.1002/ltl.20436.

7   Schulze, "Hiring Decisions that Can Make or Break the Grandest Strategies"

8   BrainyQuote®, "Charles Kettering Quotes," https://www.brainyquote.com/quotes/charles_kettering_181210.

9   "The single biggest problem with communication," *CEO Magazine*, September 5, 2019, https://www.theceomagazine.com/business/management-leadership/the-single-biggest-problem-with-communication/.

10   "Nine Interesting Things You Might Not Know About King Solomon," Crosswalk, November 26, 2019, https://www.crosswalk.com/slideshows/9-interesting-things-you-might-not-know-about-solomon.html.

11   James Kerr, Legacy (London: Constable & Robinson Ltd., 2015), 80.

12   Kerr, Legacy, 46.

13   Simran Mohanty, "Top 30 Customer Service Facts and Statistics for 2021," SmartKarrot, October 12, 2020, https://www.smartkarrot.com/resources/blog/customer-service-facts/.

14   "Temple of Jerusalem: Judaism," Encyclopedia Britannica, https://www.britannica.com/topic/Temple-of-Jerusalem.

15   Mary Omatiga, "When was the last time the Patriots missed the playoffs?" NBC Sports, November 15, 2020, https://sports.nbcsports.com/2020/11/15/when-was-the-last-time-the-patriots-missed-the-playoffs/.

16   Jean-Pierre Isbouts, "The wealthy, wise reign of King Solomon made Israel prosper," National Geographic, January 4, 2019, https://www.nationalgeographic.com/culture/people-in-the-bible/story-king-solomon-wise-temple/.

17   Jim Collins, How the Mighty Fall (Boulder, CO: Jim Collins, 2009), 13.

18   J. Peterson, "The offering ... the example of King David," Help Me with Bible Study, http://helpmewithbiblestudy.org/11Church/TitheTheOfferingKingDavid_Peterson.aspx#sthash.z95skgev.dpbs.

19   Sam Chand, Bigger, Faster Leadership: Lessons from the Builders of the Panama Canal (Nashville, TN: Thomas Nelson, 2017), 8.

20   Chand, Bigger, Faster Leadership, 45-46.

21   John S. Knox, "Solomon," Ancient History Encyclopedia, https://www.ancient.eu/solomon/.

22   Chand, Bigger, Faster Leadership, 40.

23   Excerpt from Mission Drift cited by Robert Ferguson, "The Silent Crisis of Mission Drift," Ferguson Values, June 10, 2016, https://www.fergusonvalues.com/2016/06/the-silent-crisis-of-mission-drift/.

24   Scott Gleeson, "Pickleball, the country's fastest growing sport, is also popular in this jail," USA Today , June 27, 2018, https://www.usatoday.com/story/sports/2018/06/27/pickleball-countrys-fastest-growing-sport-also-popular-cook-county-jail/718232002/.

25   Morgan Lee, "Why Did Harvard and the YMCA Stray From Their Christian Roots?" The Christian Post, February 26, 2014, https://www.christianpost.com/news/why-did-harvard-and-the-ymca-ditch-christianity.html.

26   "Interesting Facts About Solomon's Temple," BibleCharts.org, http://www.biblecharts.org/oldtestament/interestingfactsaboutsolomonstemple.pdf.

27   "Temple of Jerusalem," Britannica.com.

28   Aaron Dodson, "The forgotten history of Puma basketball," The Undefeated, February 5, 2019, https://theundefeated.com/features/the-forgotten-history-of-Puma-basketball/.

29   Scott Gleeson, "Reports: Potential top NBA draft pick Marvin Bagley III signs with Puma, spurns Nike," USA Today, June 15, 2018, https://www.usatoday.com/story/sports/nba/2018/06/15/marvin-bagley-nba-draft-picks-Puma-over-nike/704626002/.

30   Alex Nino Gheciu, "How LaMelo Ball Can Help PUMA Disrupt the Basketball Shoe Space," Complex Canada, December 4, 2020, https://www.complex.com/sneakers/2020/12/lamelo-ball-Puma-basketball-shoe-space.

31   Gheciu, "How LaMelo Ball Can Help PUMA Disrupt the Basketball Shoe Space."

32   "The Jewish Temples: The First Temple – Solomon's Temple," Jewish Virtual Library, https://www.jewishvirtuallibrary.org/the-first-temple-solomon-s-temple.

33   Bigger, Faster Leadership, 46.

34   "9 Interesting Things You Might Not Know About King Solomon."

35   Vijay Govindarajan, "How Disney Found Its Way Back to Creative Success," Harvard Business Review, June 3, 2016, https://hbr.org/2016/06/how-disney-found-its-way-back-to-creative-success.

36   Peter Fisk, "Bob Iger's ride of a lifetime … he made Disney a shining example of how large corporations can reinvent themselves for a digital world," Genius Works, March 2, 2020, https://www.thegeniusworks.com/2020/03/disney-became-a-shining-example-of-how-large-corporations-can-reinvent-themselves-for-a-digital-world-bob-iger-was-the-man-who-made-it-happen/.

37   Masters of Scale podcast with Reid Hoffman, June 27, 2017, transcript at https://mastersofscale.com/reed-hastings-culture-shock/.

38   Elon Musk, "Master Plan, Part Deux," July 20, 2016, Tesla blog, https://www.tesla.com/blog/master-plan-part-deux.

39   "Solomon," Ancient History Encyclopedia.

40   "Solomon," Ancient History Encyclopedia.